THE JAR COMPENDIUM

Get To Know Various Beginner-Friendly Spell Jar Recipes And The Fundamentals Of Using Witchcraft To Address Issues In Your Life

By

BLANCHE RODGERS

BLANCHE RODGERS © Copyright 2022. All Rights Reserved.

The publication is sold with the idea that the publisher is not required to render accounting, officially permitted or otherwise qualified services. This document is geared towards providing exact and reliable information concerning the topic and issue covered. If advice is necessary, legal or professional, a practiced individual in the profession should be ordered.

- From a Declaration of Principles which was accepted and approved equally by a Committee of the American Bar Association and a Committee of Publishers and Associations.

In no way is it legal to reproduce, duplicate, or transmit any part of this document in either electronic means or printed format. Recording of this publication is strictly prohibited, and any storage of this document is not allowed unless with written permission from the publisher—all rights reserved.

The information provided herein is stated to be truthful and consistent. Any liability, in terms of inattention or otherwise, by any usage or abuse of any policies, processes, or directions contained within is the sole and utter responsibility of the recipient reader. Under no circumstances will any legal responsibility or blame be held against the publisher for any reparation, damages, or monetary loss due to the information herein, either directly or indirectly.

Respective authors own all copyrights not held by the publisher.

The information herein is offered for informational purposes solely and is universal as so. The presentation of the information is without a contract or any guarantee assurance.

The trademarks that are used are without any consent, and the publication of the trademark is without permission or backing by the trademark owner. All trademarks and brands within this book are for clarifying purposes only and are owned by the owners themselves, not affiliated with thi

Table of Contents

INTRODUCTION 6
BASIC WITCHCRAFT PRACTICES 8
    Who is a witch? 9
    Creating a witchy environment or spell casting 12
    Creating a magical spells casting circle 18
    How to build a ritual magical witch altar 21
INTRODUCTION TO SPELL CASTING 28
    Spell fundamentals 28
    Who is capable of casting a spell? 32
    Spell components 33
    The procedure for casting love spells 36
    Simple spells for protection against negative energy 38
    How to cast powerful binding spells with the freezer spells 49
    NEW HOUSE SPELLS 55
CAST STRONG SPELLS WITH THE JAR 61
    What is a witch bottle? 62
    Why would you want to make a modern witch bottle? 64
    Jars for spell casting 66
    Witch bottles: all you need to know 68
    Spell jars 74
    The crucial elements that make up a jar spell 81
    The key to successfully casting your spell with a jar! 83
    What should you do with your spell jar after casting your spell? 98
    How to get rid of the remains of the spell jar 105
AUTHENTIC RECIPES FOR JAR SPELLS 107

Self-love spell jar 109
Love spell jar... 110
Love jar spell recipe 112
Happiness spell jar 115
Happy home spell jar 116
Good luck jar spell.. 118
Calming spell jar 119
Sleep spell jar 121
Good health spell jar 122
Recipe for a money spell jar 124
Money spell jar or abundance spell jar 126
Business abundance jar spell 128
Jars of spells to increase productivity 130
Jar containing protection spell 131
Jar of curses for the defense of the home 132
Spell jar to make people back off 134
Protection and breaking curses jar spells... 136
Lemon freezer spell:... 138
Freezer binding spell 141

EVERYTHING ABOUT CORRESPONDENCE 143
Various groups to select items from 145
Essential tools for spells 154

CONCLUSION 162

INTRODUCTION

It would appear that putting spells in bottles is the current trend in the witchy world. Perhaps you've even given one of them a shot. Could things have turned out okay? Or maybe it didn't. When it comes to doing magic in a jar, there are a few dos and don'ts that I've picked up along the way that I'd like to share with you. In this book, I will instruct you on how to cast potent jar spells and share some of my favorite love, money, and protection magic jar formulas with you.

The universe can help you get where you want to go to enhance your financial status, obtain protection, or make someone fall completely in love with you. Continue reading to find out more information! Intrigued?

For many decades, people have been studying new strategies to materialize things like luck, love, money, health, and protection. These techniques have been passed down from generation to generation.

Witches have used bottles and jars to claim their power and boost the energy behind their goals since the 17th century. This practice stems from the concept that one can bring their desires into reality if one can channel their energy properly. The greatest thing is that you don't require any unique magical powers to accomplish your goal! You can bring to you anything you focus your attention on, and jars and bottles can assist you in doing so more effectively.

Even if you've never created a spell jar, "The Jar Spells Compendium" will provide you with all the information required to make potent concoctions in jars.

Let's get started!

BASIC WITCHCRAFT PRACTICES

There has been a revival of interest in astrology, moon rituals, seasonal living, and witchcraft since the mid-20th century. You can discover a ton of witchy posts shared by women on social media, and it's past time they aggressively seized the term "witch." You'll also see that these ladies are immersing themselves in a range of aesthetics, rituals, and forms of magic.

Some believe it magically draws from the energy field surrounding us, while others think it connects to the spirit realm known as the "otherworld."

Most Wiccans practice magic because they think it enables them to interact with the spirit world. The phrase "otherworld" is frequently used to describe this world. They emphasize that magic must not have negative effects and use it to heal themselves and others and find a new house or job, among other things. Those who walk this road are motivated to concentrate on self-improvement and empowerment because they believe those who practice magic undergo alterations similar to those induced by their surroundings.

Who is a witch?

Because contrary to what a great number of novels and movies have asserted throughout the years, a witch is not a lady with a green face who cackles as she hunches over her cauldron working wicked magic and flies her broomstick around at night, terrorizing innocent victims.

This is only a caricature of a witch, that terrible man who feared witches and their power and sought to stigmatize and vilify women who were invented and propagated.

A witch is an independent woman who is untamed, unrepentant, and deeply rooted in her authority. She connects to her inner magic to leave the spiritual realm, enter the physical realm, creates, and manifest. She coexists with nature and the Goddess in her daily activities and work. Additionally, she lives an independent life.

Women worldwide realize their holiness, which has long been hidden and vilified.

A regular gathering of witches is known as a "coven" in common parlance. Some witches say that a coven must have at least three members but no fewer than thirteen.

How did the original meaning of witchcraft change?

Before the witch trials, when witch panic swept across Europe, witches were integral to every community. They were the healers, midwives, sages, and practitioners of ancient medicine. Using their comprehensive understanding of plants, herbs, and energies, they produced cures for the ill, helped pregnant women, and advised on the best time to plant or harvest crops.

If you owned a cat, were informed about medications, knew how to avoid becoming pregnant, or could read cards and predict the future, you were accused of being a witch. In a nutshell, every strong, independent woman was called a witch. Even while the Holocaust gained a lot of attention, the witch hunts resulted in the deaths of many more women. The millions of women slain and tormented by the patriarchy are rarely mentioned (mostly Christian men).

You might think that this is over, but it isn't. Particularly in African cultures, children are still accused of witchcraft as though it were a vice that required punishment. Don't give up on your magic and craft because of your fear. Fear was used centuries ago to control people, the land, and modern capitalist institutions, to divide women from their power, and it still is today.

Everyone has access to witchcraft.

The witch of today might be found in a variety of forms. Because there are so many different types of witches and practices of modern witchcraft, you may pick and choose the aspects of witchcraft most interest you. No rules apply in this situation.

Even if a woman does not follow "conventional" witchcraft practices or doesn't have a lengthy history of engaging in the craft, she might still be considered a witch.

As a result, I want you to know that you are a witch just like any other woman, whether you enjoy adding crystals to your bath, giving yourself and your friends regular oracle readings, participating in full moon rituals, or combining earth-sourced ingredients to make mouthwatering dishes in the kitchen.

Creating a witchy environment or spell casting

Even while it is possible to cast a spell in any location, I like to create a certain atmosphere for myself when I practice. This isn't always required, but I find that doing it helps me get into the spirit of the magic I'm performing.

When I'm in the mood to practice witchcraft, I have a greater capacity for amassing power. It would be beneficial if you attempted to enter the spirit of the spell you are currently casting automatically and subconsciously to produce something truly powerful. This is true for the majority of witches.

In general, novice witches do not have access to many tools or a fully-functioning spell workroom; nevertheless, it is not always necessary to have any of these things. There are many ways to imbue a location with a "witchy aura" without spending much money.

The calling of a witchy environment in which to cast spells can be achieved in a number of different ways; the following are five of my favorites.

1. LISTEN TO MUSIC

Others need perfect silence, while some witches like to focus on background music playing. A good song helps me when I need to get into the witchy mindset to work on spells.

I use one of the many different playlists I've made when I practice. The first features more haunting, traditional Irish music, while the second is more bohemian and heavily incorporates Fleetwood Mac. I also offer a playlist of rougher sounds for spellwork with a darker, more intensive theme.

If you want to listen to music while you exercise a hobby of yours, take some time to put together a strong playlist. Make sure it flows naturally and stays true to the spirit of the spell you are casting.

It is quite frustrating to have to stop listening to a song in the middle of it and look for another one, which may completely ruin the atmosphere. I advise you to put together your music before casting your circle so you won't be interrupted while working on something vital.

Playing music is a great first step if you're having problems getting into the spirit of your spellwork. I enter a trance much more quickly when music plays, especially if the songs are meaningful to me that day.

2. INCENSE MUST BE LIT.

Utilizing one's senses properly is a necessary step in the process of producing a creepy environment. During spell work, the scent is significant, even on a subconscious level, and it assists me in maintaining my attention.

When it comes to the sense of smell, burning incense is by far my favorite way to get into the mood for casting spells. I choose my incense's scent based on what I like to smell and what aromas are appropriate for my ritual.

Since I burn incense for the entirety of my training sessions, I always ensure a good supply on hand.

3. BRING IN THE VARIOUS COMPONENTS.

Using the senses when casting spells is crucial, but the elements must also be considered. After all, the most essential aspects of witchcraft revolve on the four cardinal direction.

Before I start training, I prefer to set up my environment to include all the elements. I believe that maintaining a balance between the elements helps me to remain focused and attentive on both a spiritual and physical level. In addition, the elements assist me in more successfully grounding my energies.

For instance, I enjoy placing an indoor plant (representing soil), a cup of water or an indoor fountain (representing water), several lit candles (representing fire), and some incense on the table where I'm working (air). When I require a lot of circulation, I will sometimes use a fan instead of the air conditioner, and when there is a warm wind outside, I will open the window.

You can substitute anything you want for each ingredient if you want. Despite the fact that this element does not have to be flawless, it is quite important to guarantee that you have a connection with all of the components and that the proportions of each component are fairly balanced.

Depending on the spell you are casting, you can add more of a particular element if you think it will help you, although this is unnecessary.

4. MAKE A SMALL ALTAR

When they perform their rituals, some witches always use the same altar in the same place. I consider myself to have a more fluid personality.

Regardless of the circumstances, erecting an altar in your practice is almost always an excellent method to bring a witchy air to the proceedings. You can carry out this ritual using a permanent altar or a table that will only be used once during the ceremony before being stored away.

I like to spread out a cloth (I use something similar), place candles in each of the four corners, and then add other objects that hold special meaning to my altar. I may include a crystal ball or a deck of Tarot cards in some circumstances while choosing a salt dish, a figurine, or crystals in others.

You can arrange as few or as many things as you choose on your altar. No particular number is right or wrong. When you're out shopping, I think it's important to keep an eye out for things that catch your eye and interest you. These shouldn't necessarily be the priciest goods but rather those that add to the room's ambiance.

Everything in this place serves a function! Your capacity to feel witchy will directly correlate to the growth of your energy throughout time. This indicates that your spells will have a greater degree of success.

5. DRESS APPROPRIATELY

Last but not least, when I am working on my craft, I dress in a particular manner. It's great for getting me in the mood when I need it!

Although I enjoy being at ease, I almost always dress in all black to keep my mental state as uncluttered as possible.

There are distinctions between people. Depending on the kind of spell they are doing, some witches enjoy donning various costumes, such as Victorian, edgy, or trendy garb. Some people want to kick back and relax. Although many witches choose wearing black, white, or neutral tones, others find that working with color and the connotations connected with certain spells helps them feel more in control of their magic.

Determine which types of clothing look and feel the greatest when worn by you. If you try a few different techniques to solve the problem, it is not an issue!

Because everything that occurs during the casting of a spell has some association, how you appear and feel will bring a certain energy to your practice, and I believe that clothing has a vital role to play in this. Because of this, I believe that it is quite significant.

Creating a magical spells casting circle

Your altar and casting circle play crucial roles in the effectiveness and potency of your magic spells. I want to cover the three components in this section:

Your altar

You cast spells at your altar, keeping all of your magical supplies. A basic fold-out coffee table or a specially built marble table made for witchcraft might serve this purpose.

The candles are placed on the altar, which serves as a platform to arrange any items needed to begin spellcasting. As you accumulate more items over time and infuse the altar with your power with each spell, your altar will gradually grow more and more embellished and hallowed.

You will greatly benefit from a blessed, sacred, and magical environment where you can practice your magic.

Your magic circle

Circles, pentagrams, and anchor symbols are regularly combined, increasing their power and importance. In general, your circle can be on your altar. On your altar, your circle is where you cast spells. It is where you concentrate your attention.

The circle's purpose is to bring all your energy close to you and channel it into the spell you intend to cast. Before you attempt to cast a spell, you go around the circle and sprinkle holy Water. Incense is another method that can be used to cleanse the circle.

Your anchor objects

Anchor items can take the form of tiny charms, pendants, or other objects that are significant to the user and that can be used to evoke feelings and energy inside the user related to the anchor object in question. You were given a miniature carved dragon as a present from an old friend, and this item serves as a representation of the Fire spirit.

Think about the things you can discover in your immediate surroundings that you could use to symbolize the five elements of magic: earth, air, fire, water, and spirit. Consider how you could use these things. Then, to connect your circle and yourself with the force of nature, select a specific anchor object for each of the five spirits, and set it around your circle. This will complete the connection.

How to build a ritual magical witch altar

When you hear the word altar, images of a bland, musty church altar with pillar candles on top may come to mind. A Wiccan altar or pagan altar, however, predates those found in modern churches. Witches' altars are another name for these altars.

In the past, witches used these places of worship to worship the Goddess, pray, cast spells, meditate, and read tarot cards. However, anybody can make a witch altar; you do not need to be a practicing witch in order to do so. Your sacred altar can reflect the energy and life you're calling in—your dreams, beliefs, and ambitions.

It's a lovely site to use as an anchor throughout the day and to base your daily practice on. However, that could be for you. You may meditate, do yoga, conduct a full moon ritual, perform an egg cleanse, or sit quietly and take in the solitude. Performing your morning or evening rituals at your altar is another option. At this time, your physical form, mental state, and spirit all converge, and you begin to pour yourself back into your cup.

How does one construct an altar in witchcraft?

When it comes to creating a personal witch altar, there are no rules to follow at all! Altars are private places that should be used to authentically express one's core beliefs and areas of focus regarding personal growth. When it comes to matters of appearance and possessions, different witches place varying amounts of importance on certain factors.

Some altars are crafted from wood, while others have been built on lovely trays, coffee table tops, shelves, windowsills, or even miniature shoe boxes as their foundation. It's up to you whether you want to keep it simple or go all out. When deciding what will serve as the foundation of your witch altar and when you first start putting it together, let your intuition lead you.

Creating a witch altar

It has been established that no one approach is better or worse than any other to construct your sacred altar. Enjoy yourself and the experience. Things need to be shifted around. Always go with your first instinct. Refreshing your altar with new items to which you regularly feel connected is a great way to make it reflect the woman you are evolving into.

According to Wiccan custom, the side of a witch's altar that faces left is considered the feminine side, while the side that faces right is considered the masculine side. You may find it beneficial to arrange materials like as a chalice or cauldron on the left of your working area, and your wand and athame on the right. This is your "working space," where you carry out your witchcraft or any other sacred rituals; the center is where the Goddess and God meet.

Another common practice for building a witch's altar is to orient it such that it faces in the direction that feels the most meaningful to you (north, east, south, or west).

How to style your altar according to the seasons

The Wheel of the Year, which includes eight different feasts or Sabbats that honor the earth's four seasons, governs the lives of Pagans and Wiccans.

We have four quarter-point Sabbats as well as our cross-quarter Sabbats.

The festivals of the cross-quarter (fire):

- Imbolc (February 1st) (February 1st)
- Beltane (May 1st) (May 1st)
- Lammas (August 1st) (August 1st)

- Samhain (October 31st) (October 31st)

The festivals of the quarter-point (solar):

- Spring Solstice (20th – 23rd March)
- summer's equinox (20th – 23rd June)
- Autumnal New Year (20th – 23rd September)
- Christmas Day (20th – 23rd December)

It is a great way to rejuvenate your altar regularly and call upon and enjoy the natural cycles and seasons to decorate it following these Sabbats. Think about the colors, things smells, and themes connected with each of these seasons, and consider what they mean to you personally. It would be nice to commemorate the festival of Imbolc with something as simple as a few crocuses arranged in a vase. Similarly, it would be lovely to mark the Spring Equinox with an ornamental egg, and it would be lovely to honor the Winter Solstice with a branch of holly.

Keeping your witch altar safe

Here are some techniques for shielding your altar against evil spirits and harmful energy:

- It is appropriate to light a white or black candle (at least once a day)
- Keep some black salt on hand.
- Add a crystal of tourmaline or obsidian.

How to purify your altar

Since your altar serves as your temple, it is crucial to cleanse it frequently. As a result, cleanse it frequently, and do it just before performing any rituals or spells. Clean it up and remove any dust. Dead plants or flowers should be replaced. Give it lots of love and attention.

Burning palo santo or sage is an effective way to purge the environment of any negative or stale energy. If you are looking for an easier and more sanitary method to clean your altar, try placing a few drops of sage oil in a diffuser and allowing it to work its magic to cleanse the air. During the ritual, you are free to leave this turned on.

Practice these rituals at your witch altar.

You might want to perform the following rituals at your altar:

- word work
- a full-moon or new-moon ritual
- Meditation
- Yoga
- Reading
- Chanting
- Prayer
- Self-care
- drawing tarot or oracle cards
- Journaling

- establishing new objectives
- making empowering statements
- Creating
- Writing
- Visualizing
- Cleansing

You should make every effort to acquire all of the necessary items before beginning any kind of ritual. This will ensure that you are prepared for the experience and able to give it your whole attention.

In an ideal world, the key is to make as much use of your altar each day as you possibly can. Your work will benefit from regular practice, and it will also help you create the changes and aspirations you want in your life.

INTRODUCTION TO SPELL CASTING

People are naturally curious; thus, it hardly ever goes a day without someone asking you about spells. A spell is a mental act that tells the universe what you need or want most. It's a way to craft a spell and make an effort to attract the things your heart truly desires while blending thought, symbols, and playfulness. The Universe answers our request and helps us get what we need when we do this.

Spell fundamentals

Let's start by going over some basics. What precisely is the definition of a spell? A magickal formula is known as a spell, and it is used to exert influence on another entity, such as the result of a certain set of events. You are free to make these formulae as straightforward or complicated as you see fit. A spell may be as easy as reciting a few words, or it can be as complicated as an extended ritual that involves a range of different features and pieces. The level of complexity that a spell reaches depends on how it is cast.

Or, to put it another way, a spell is a magical recipe. Consider them as a base for implementing or partaking in magical rituals. Making pizza dough is simple, but making macarons or other baked goods requires more effort. It needs time and practice to finish a spell properly, just like cooking. This is akin to how food is prepared.

Magick

Next, a practical definition of magick must be offered. A force used to affect an event's course, outcome, or other aspects is a typical definition of magick. It is customary to describe this power as the energy one can employ to exert control over or influence another. The practice of magick nearly usually involves a person's will or intent in some form.

The energy is referred to as magick. If you're starting, you might be wondering what this means. In that it will move in the direction of less resistance, it functions similarly to other types of energy. In other words, when a spell is performed, its energy will move along the "smoothest" path, the path with the least friction.

For instance, if the goal of a spell was to acquire money and the caster found five dollars in his pocket as a result of casting the spell, we can say that the spell was successful since its desired result—the caster acquired money—was met. Although the person who cast the magic probably had other ideas about how the activity should be completed, having the money on hand made the task go much more quickly. This is one of the most common reasons why people jump to the conclusion that a spell will not be successful in achieving the objective it was cast for.

The majority of people grossly underestimate the difficulty of magic. The presented example demonstrates the importance of intention and phrasing in magick, which is crucial to learn.

Intentions

Intentions? Why do you say that, exactly? And why are they so important? Your intentions are what you want to happen in the scenario or what results you want the spell to have. It is essential to be as specific as possible while figuring out someone's aim. Things might not go as planned if one is not explicit.

Similar to the previous example, the goal was to build financial riches. The money was discovered to have been left in a pocket, and as a result, it was obtained, resulting in the successful casting of the spell.

What are some things that, in your opinion, could have been done otherwise to produce a different or more agreeable result, keeping this information in mind?

It is possible to have more direct intentions for the goal one wishes to accomplish when we step back and think about the motives. When we do this, we become aware that it is possible to develop intentions for a more specific objective. For instance, if casting the spell is done with a specific goal (such as increasing money to cover one's upcoming expenses for the next three weeks), that should be the motivation behind doing it. Incredibly clear and precise

One must also refrain from performing any action that would stop the spell from working. What exactly is meant by this at this point may be puzzling to you. To put it more simply, one must also be willing to exert effort to fulfill the spell's target or goals. This is why: Spells are nothing more than a way to facilitate travel by opening doorways. Therefore, one may anticipate finding new employment or working additional hours at their existing job to meet this need if the goal of their spell is to amass enough money to cover future bills for the next three weeks. Another excellent alternative is ensuring one is prepared to act on potential future opportunities that may arise and fulfill the wish expressed in the magickal work conducted. A great strategy to increase one's chances of success would be to do this.

<u>Who is capable of casting a spell?</u>

In a nutshell, the answer is anyone and everyone.

Have you ever desired something so intensely that it consumed your thoughts (like a present for your birthday, for instance)? Many people have already done so without even knowing. So, you were able to obtain it. Despite the possibility that it was not carried out on a "great scale," the intention you put into obtaining what you want was a type of spell.

Will my charm have any effect? When a similar spell is casted between two people, particularly one that is in the opposite direction of what you would expect it to go, there is a possibility that your spell will not come to light or will not take place in the manner in which it was intended to. That is dependent on a lot of different things.

Casting a spell requires practice and instruction, like learning how to ride a bike. This is of even greater significance when working with more complicated spells. This indicates that someone who has been training for a long period would most likely be successful than someone who has just begun to cast spells. Someone practicing for a shorter time may not be able to cast spells at all.

As with most endeavors, the results will be significantly improved upon completing further practice and investing additional time to get the duties done. In addition to some circumstances, some people are naturally gifted than others. When casting spells, certain individuals need to exert more effort or concentration than others.

Spell components

Spells are complex beasts, which is why so many spellcasters use Intelligence, Wisdom or Vharisma to cast. Spells require physical components for them to work and we'll be breaking down those components in this section.

If you look at one of your spells, you'll see a line that reads "components" beneath the name of the spell, and then you could see a V, an S, and M, or a combination of those three letters.

These stand for:

- Verbal
- Somatic
- Material

They are the structure of spells.

Verbal

Let's start with verbal. Most spells are going to have that V listed, as most require you to say something in order to cast. Some sort of chance or magic phrase, something that creates sound that activates the magic.

If your spell uses a verbal component, it has to be spoken out into the world twice; it's why silence is such an effective spell against magic users. Write that down.

Somatic

Now that S stands for somatic. Somatic means that it requires a gesture. It might not be a complex gesture, but if the spell you were trying to cast uses a somatic component, you're going to have to have at least one hand free in order to make that finger wiggle or hand wave happen.

Material

Finally, there's M for materials. Sometimes your spell requires an actual object channel, the spell through to be cast. If so your spell will list exactly what items it requires next to that label M.

Maybe it's something simple, like a small feather for Feather Fall or it could require components with a price tag, like Raise Dead, which needs a diamond worth at least 500 gold and that diamond then gets consumed.

Once the spell is complete. Every Spell will tell you what it means and whether or not that material gets used up at the end of casting. I know what you're thinking: "I need feathers for Feather Fall, a caterpillar cocoon for Polymorph, or bat guano for Fireball."

How am I supposed to keep track of all these materials? Well, good news. You have two options to help with that. You can choose to use a component pouch which acts as an all-in-one hub that's assumed to always contain the majority of the time materials you need.

Or you can choose to use a spellcasting focus.

A spellcasting focus is a single item that a spellcaster uses as a kind of divining or channeling rod that replaces the need for those minor material components.

Focuses will differ depending on your class. An Arcane focus is an item like a wand or an orb, or a staff that is used to channel the Arcane powers of Wizard, a Warlock or a Sorcerer. A Druidic focus is something nature-based, like a feather, antlers, or another wander stuff that's used to channel the powers of nature.

Cleric use their whole symbol as a focus and bards can use their musical instrument. Whatever you choose to use as a focus pick an item that has meaning for your character.

Having a focus is no longer a magical "Now, I never have to use materials again," panacea. If your spell has a material cost specified in the spell, it needs expensive components that can't be replicated by a focus.

Whatever ruby dust, diamond, or Enchanted bowl is called for in the spell, you must still have on hand. Sometimes to the point of consuming.

The focus takes care of the smaller stuff, but not the financial burden. As always, please read your Spell's thoroughly before attempting to cast. All the information is right there. Telling you, whether it must be spoken aloud just to collated wildly or cost an honor to be completed.

The procedure for casting love spells

Are you jilted by a would-be lover? Try a good old-fashioned hex, and change his mind. You will need the following items:

- Pink candle
- Vase
- Pink flowers like roses or gardenias.

Step 1.

After sunset, light a candle and place it next to the vase.

Step 2.

Say aloud: "I ask the power of love and light to bring the opportunities for romance."

Step 3.

Next, recite: "I affirm that I participate in love and that I am worthy of love." Legend holds that this spell works best on the Friday night before a full moon.

Step 4

Next, repeat the following mantra: "I am open to love and ask that it come to me for the greater good."

Step 5.

Finish by muttering, "So be it and so it is."

Step 6:

Extinguish the candle. Before doing the spell again, give it at least a month.

Step 7.

Leave the flowers around until they wither. Your new love should bloom after they've entirely dried up. If it doesn't, try once again, but use a finer vase.

Simple spells for protection against negative energy

We are aware that energy underlies everything in our world. New energy is produced through words, thoughts, and deeds, and these three factors alter existing energies. Failure to secure them causes our homes and places of business to be as susceptible to assaults by malicious energy as we are to becoming the subject of such assaults. Because of this, we will learn easy spells for protection against bad energy, which we can employ at home and in our business.

Complaining nonstop, dirt, clutter, foul language, useless objects, and negative thoughts are the primary contributors that turn our home on Earth into a depressing place and drain our vitality, causing us to become ill, and driving us to madness, depression, or even death. These are the primary factors that turn our home on Earth into a depressing place. These are the primary contributors to the darkness that pervades our planet, which serves as our home.

To avoid issues of this sort, it is necessary to infuse our home and place of workplace with good energy and to pray for the presence and protection of the Goddess.

However, we do not have to lay this responsibility completely in the hands of the Goddess; rather, we should adopt a variety of preventative measures to ensure the safety of the areas.

Take a look at these 10 simple spells that might be of assistance to you in the process of safeguarding your home or place of business from any energy infiltration that could lead to the introduction of bad influences or low energies:

1. SUMMON THE GODDESS USING SPIRALS

A design in the shape of a spiral or an item that is fashioned in the shape of a spiral that is put in the doorway of a house has the ability to divert undesirable energies away from the house. The spiral, which is an old Celtic emblem, features prominently in Wiccan rituals and practices. When approaching from the inside, use the same spiral as before, but turn it so that the right side is facing you.

It is believed in Wicca that the spiral is symbolic of the power that the Mother Goddess has. You will only have any chance of success if you cast this one simple spell as a safeguard.

Despite the fact that there are more double and triple spirals, the one that is illustrated here is the one that, under the circumstances, makes the most sense. The act of turning to the left is symbolic of "banishment," which purges one's body of any destructive energy. When turned to face the right, it symbolizes "attraction," which is the attraction to the power and protection of the Goddess. When turned to face the left, it depicts "repulsion."

Drawing spirals in the air with your magic wand or your fingertip as you go into a new place or over items as you come across them or obtain them is a fantastic method that can be applied in a variety of settings and scenarios. While you are doing this, you are simultaneously making a request to the Goddess to be with you so that you may either attract beneficial energies or drive away bad ones.

2. FILL A GLASS WITH WATER AND COARSE SALT.

This specific kind of witchcraft is highly popular among its practitioners. Casting this easy spell, which only takes a few minutes to finish, will allow you to shield yourself from harm and protect you from potential harm. Put some coarse salt and water in a glass or jar, preferably one that is crystal and has never been used before. The perfect container for this would be one that is made of crystal. Be careful to stir the mixture with the wooden spoon counterclockwise to the direction the clock is facing. Keep it in the foyer of your home or place of business, preferably behind the door, so that it may take up any negative energy that may be present when people enter and exit the premises. This will allow it to perform its job more effectively. Take the glass out of the cabinet once a month and empty its contents into one of the streams or rivers in the vicinity. The act of adding water and coarse salt to it, giving it a whirl after each addition, and then placing it in the lobby should be repeated as many times as necessary.

3. FASHION YOURSELF A PROTECTIVE AMULET

This custom of wearing an amulet for protection is said to have originated in the Mediterranean area. It is designed to protect the entrance to your property as well as provide protection for any and all exits. Find an old key (the longer it has been around, the better), wrap it in a ribbon of red, and then hang it on the back of the front door to perform this simple protection spell. The longer the key has been around, the better.

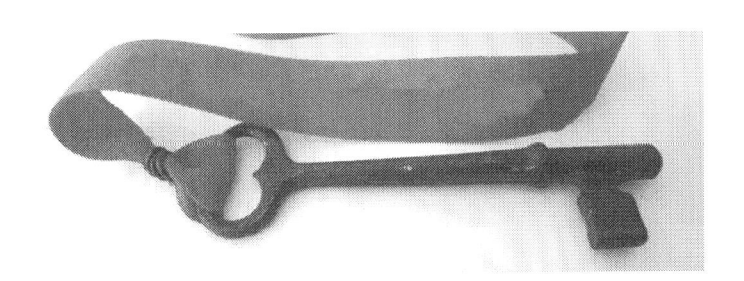

4. PREPARE A SPELL BOTTLE.

In order to perform this straightforward kind of magical defense, you will need a witch's bottle. The Witches' Bottle, which is sometimes referred to as a Spell Bottle, has been around for a very long time in a variety of shapes and has been put to use for a wide range of purposes.

You should fill a frosted jar that you have prepared with needles, nails, and any other potentially harmful materials. Put the lid on the jar so that no one else can get into it, and then put it in a prominent place in your house so that everyone can see it.

Never reveal either what it is or what it says to anybody else. This is a powerful amulet that will protect both your home and your place of business from being targeted by bad spirits. Bury it when you no longer need to use it or when you realize that it has already absorbed enough energy to meet your requirements and you can do without it.

5. BEFRIEND THE ELEMENTALS

This simple defensive spell need to be turned into a requirement of some kind.

Be warned that if you have plants growing in plant pots within your house, elementals may choose to make those plant pots their homes. You may gain the favor of a Gnome, which represents the land, a Sylph, which represents the air, an Undine, which represents the water, or a Salamander if you put colorful jelly beans, blackberries, or tiny berries in the pots (representing the fire). There is a common misconception that the mere existence of a fountain constitutes an open invitation to the Undines. They assert that the home is protected from harm and filled with pleasure due to the fact that they are cheerful.

There is a kind of ethereal entity known as the Elementals, and they are said to call the sphere of the Earth home. However, even if we can hardly make out their shapes, we are still able to feel them. We are able to converse with elementals due to the fact that they are also manifestations of energy in the same way that we are.

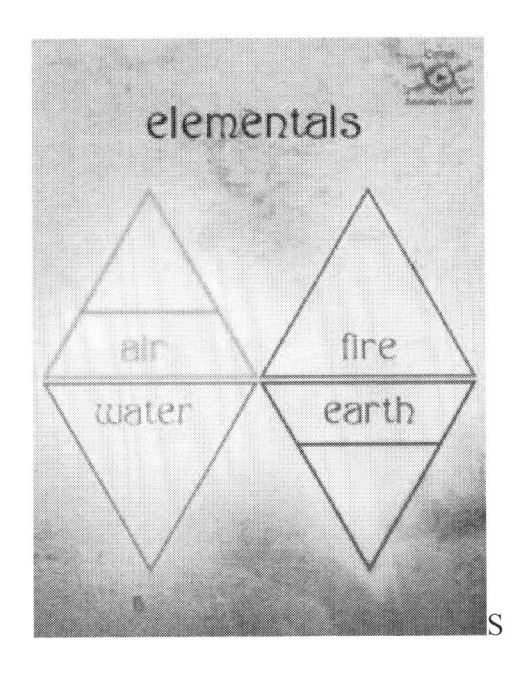

elementals

air · fire
water · earth

6. CONSTRUCT AN ALTAR

In the event that you still haven't produced one after all this time, of course. Construct an altar to pay homage to the deity or gods with whom you identify the most, and be sure to maintain it as neat and organized as possible. Make room for your imagination to go wild, and while it's running, think about the symbols that symbolize these gods.

As was just said, make sure that your altar is spotless and well-organized. For instance, while constructing an altar to the goddess Venus, it is customary to incorporate flowers and shells in the construction of the altar. On the other side, it is traditional to lay some dirt and leaves on an altar that is dedicated to the goddess Gaia. In addition, we really value the inclusion of photographs and any other types of representations.

7. USE THE PIN BELL AND SING MANTRAS

In order to cast a spell in the most efficient manner possible, you should make use of your own voice as the medium. This link between the phrases "spell" and "enchantment" and the performance of magical activities was not made by accident; rather, it was done on purpose. This basic protection spell calls for the use of a "pin bell" and a mantra of your choosing as its essential components.

The pin bell is a traditional Tibetan bell that is used as an instrument for energizing the surrounding region as well as detecting the frequency of vibrations. Its purpose is twofold: first, it energizes the area, and second, it provides a measurement of the You may use the pin bell in a number of different places all throughout your house or place of workplace to assess whether or not everything is in working condition.

When the energies are at their greatest and most stable levels, the sound of the bell will be "smooth" and steady throughout the whole ringing. The sound of the pin bell will be "shaky" and unstable in the event that there is any kind of disturbance.

You may determine if the power supply on the first shelf of a cabinet is stable by looking at it or, alternatively, by pressing the pin bell that is located on that shelf. Nevertheless, while measuring the second shelf, the sound may be a little bit unstable at times.

This will provide evidence that there is anything in the vicinity that is causing a shift in the energy. It may be an item that was gained by you dishonestly, a buildup of dust, or even some annotation of anything harmful that had been left inside of some object. All of these are possibilities. After you have identified what caused the interruption and removed the source of this energy, ring the bell one again to double check that everything is in working order.

You might also try meditating with it or chanting mantras with it. These are two alternative applications for the pin bell. You are free to experiment with playing it while reciting your preferred mantra or the sound "Om." if you so want.

8. LET IT GO

Do not gather items! Laissez-Les aller! This uncomplicated spell for personal protection need to eventually become automatic for you.

The accumulation is damaging to everyone and everything, including the many places they inhabit. Give up whatever that you no longer need since there is always going to be someone else who does.

Many people (and believe me when I say that this is more common than we may think), who gather things because they feel safe with them, do so for psychological reasons. This can place on a variety of scales, from the simple act of leaving a piece of paper in a drawer to the most severe examples of compulsive hoarding, and it may be brought on by a number of different factors.

Psychiatrists, on the other hand, do not divulge the fact that the environment in which the accumulations are formed is infused with harmful and negative energy. To be more specific, this is the reason why the lives of these individuals who accumulate are often plagued with peril, including but not limited to separation, ill health, feelings of isolation, and even death.

To put this simple protection spell into action, all that is necessary is for the target to release their grip over the situation. Everything will turn out just like it was imagined.

9. BURN INCENSE

You may cast this protection spell anytime you choose, making it the simplest of all the simple protection spells offered in this article.

Incense may be burnt to cleanse the atmosphere of any potential spiritual toxins that may be present. Sandalwood, rosemary, and lavender are all fantastic options to consider in this scenario.

Burn the incense whenever a window is left open, since this allows the air to bring in good energy and take away any bad energy that may be present. You are free to combine and experiment with various types of incense, or you may choose the one that makes you feel the most at ease and stick with it.

10. MAKE USE OF A MAGICAL BROOM

Every Witch has to have access to a Magical Broom as one of her essential tools. Make use of it to clean your home so that you can perform this simple spell in order to protect yourself. Despite the fact that you probably won't see a witch soaring through the air on a broomstick, it does not imply that brooms are nothing more than ornamental ornaments.

Consecrated brooms have the potential to cleanse an area of any bad energies that may be present there. This power may be used to clear a space. In order to achieve this, you must first take control of your broom, bless it, and then sing the following while sweeping the floor in a magical manner from the center outward while keeping your feet off the ground:

- The floor is being swept, swept, then swept once more.
- putting an end to the harmful things, the filth, and more
- May love, goodness, and health always accompany me, for the air in my house is fresh, pure, and unpolluted.

Energizing the environment with easy periods of protection

In addition to the advice presented here, you might also try sprinkling stones and crystals across your place of business or residence. Because many crystals possess various capabilities, you should experiment with various combinations to purify your environment and attract the qualities you seek.

How to cast powerful binding spells with the freezer spells

In the magical world, freeze spells have become incredibly popular recently. They are a kind of magic that works quickly and directly, making them incredibly potent. Additionally, frozen spells work well for various things, including binding, pausing or holding a situation, establishing serenity, or even stopping someone in their tracks. The history of freezing spells will be covered in this section, along with the justifications for why you can use them as long as you use them responsibly.

A freezer spell: what is it? The heart of it

A freezer spell is what it sounds like: a spell that takes advantage of the freezing qualities of your freezer. Recent years have seen a rise in their popularity among Wizards and Witches. This problem has become so pervasive that people may even say casting freezer magic is a "closed" technique. However, it's not true if you try to personalize it and carefully pick your words and parts.

Freezer's relevance in the field of magic and its history

To those who think that only a specific magical lineage can use freezer spells in their magick, I have to ask: Is it necessary for me to avoid using my stove and oven? How about candlelight? Do they also follow some ancient magic? I'm trying to make the point that some charms for the freezer employ practices from Hoodoo folk magic, including sour and sweetening jars. Such elements and techniques should be removed from your personalized freezer magic if you are worried about being accused of appropriation.

From vintage ice chests to cutting-edge freezers

I do not doubt that our ancestors used what they already possessed to create magick, cast spells, and dispense remedies. Any available household appliances and other components of their home fall under this category. Our forefathers are included when I use the phrase "our forebears." Every civilization has had and continues to have individuals with magical prowess who have been casting potent spells for centuries. What alternatives did they have for refrigeration, considering they lacked a freezer?

As per Swirl Freeze, the ability to freeze a meal for long-term storage was equally as important to the advancement of civilization as the ability to cook food with fire. The earliest people who learned how to preserve food by putting it on the ice were those who lived in more harsh climates. Over antiquity, icehouses—basically small structures containing ice and food intended to be frozen—became increasingly widely used. Ice chests were then placed there.

How do spells to freeze things work?

Let's examine the magic's internal mechanisms, shall we? Everything put inside the freezer is frozen there and only there. Also, freezing and preserving are the same. Many methods are available for casting freeze spells. However, the fridge's magic changes when we consider the numerous purposes for which spells might be cast.

Consider the case where you recently began working a more dangerous job. The working environment is unpleasant due to a coworker, and you occasionally worry about your safety. Your manager has been informed of your worries, but nothing has been done about them.

Therefore, you've decided to cast a spell that would bind this coworker like ice. Expect it to work, however, consider the time the cast will be active, and the time the binding spell will be stored in the freezer. These two elements are crucial.

For the argument, let's say that you realize things are moving too quickly for you to feel comfortable. And to a large extent, it's leading to stress, worry, or discomfort. If the procedure has already started, is there a way to either slow it down or stop it? It would help if you had freeze spells to do this magical endeavor. Consider it this way: if you want to PRESERVE anything by freezing it in place or stopping it from moving, a freezer spell will work. When you are prepared to recommence the natural flow of time, you take the spell out of the freezer and let it "defrost."

Freezer spells have MANY various uses that can be accomplished.

Most of my freezer spells research led me to conclude that their main function is to bind a specific person or situation. Even though this is most often what people intend when casting a freezer spell, this is by no means the only way one might employ a freezer in their magical work. Using the freezer in place of ice spells can accomplish several goals, including entering a different universe. The following exist in this universe.

- Freezer spells are an excellent way to maintain love and friendship.
- To maintain an employment opportunity or one's current pay
- to slow down the passage of time so that it isn't so rushed
- Take care of one's health.
- Put a stop to a potentially harmful person or circumstance by tying them up.
- When we cast our spells utilizing ice, it helps to maintain silence.
- Command of Oneself

- Attention and focus are required.
- Learning how to adjust one's behavior in response to sudden change
- Bringing some relief to a tense situation
- Extreme purification
- In ceremonies of devotion to gods and goddesses.

The "Magical Morals" Behind the Casting of Spells That Bind with Freezer Rays

It seems appropriate for me to intervene at this point and discuss the ethical ramifications of using spells to ensnare individuals in freezers. Many individuals would advise you not to interfere with someone else's free will since doing so is morally unacceptable. should let the cosmos or the gods to handle these problems.

If you believe that casting binding charms in any way violates your moral beliefs, you should refrain from doing so. The issue is that sometimes the cosmos and the gods demand that we defend ourselves from danger. If we still feel endangered despite our best efforts in the physical domain, we can always depend on magic to assist us.

Strategies and elements for the fun spell

You must have guessed that the two major components of freezer spells are water and the real freezer. Other intuitive components like fruits, flowers, odd containers, herbs, and flowers should not be discounted. Try using the freezer in other ways for your magical work as well. In a traditional casting, the target's name or details of the problem are written on a sheet of paper, which is then submerged in water and allowed to freeze.

Simple, but there are a ton of fantastic things you can do with your freezer, including the following:

Make a true magic ritual out of your kid-friendly, at-home ice-based scientific experiments. Ice cubes may be made by freezing herbs, flowers, and other things in an ice cube pan. Then give magical creatures ice cubes. I save food and other goods in the freezer for future consumption since I'm a kitchen witch.

Optional: To thaw or remove a cast freezer spell, try melting an ice cube or block using your witch's black salt. This strategy is quite effective.

Create enchanted herbal tea or coffee cubes for next meals and drinks.

Garden seeds should be stored so that they may be used the next year's growth season.

Throughout the summer, aloe vera leaves may be frozen to ease the pain of insect bites and sunburns.

For a nutritious witchy breakfast, combine individual servings of magical smoothie packets.

You've undoubtedly figured out by now that the strength of your imagination and intuitive powers are the only things that may limit your effectiveness while utilizing freezer spells or spells in general.

Freezer Spell is an alternative name for the Ice and Snow Magick Casting.

Your feelings toward employing frozen materials in your magical practices may be influenced by your ancestors who may have come from an area with more extreme winters. You can create your own using the freezer, a dependable ally. You may even buy a reasonably cost snow cone maker for your house to make the snow you need for your spells. But what occurs if you go to a place with milder weather and can no longer obtain snow, ice, or hail?

NEW HOUSE SPELLS

There are two new house spells: one for finding your dream home and one for locating a home.

You've finally reached a stage where you can purchase your own home. Congratulations! Or perhaps you need a fresh residence. In either case, you have no idea of beginning and requiring magical assistance. We have provided two new house spells for you to choose from. The first will help you purchase your dream house, and the second will locate the ideal land for your new home.

The property finder spell is the first in the list of new house spells.

Are you prepared to relocate but unsure where to buy or build a new home? Use this straightforward property locator spell to find the best location for your upcoming venture.

What you'll need is as follows:

- A map of the large area where moving a pendulum is desired (alternatively, try using a necklace with a charm, pendant, or crystal on it).
- Rosemary oil (optional but helpful)
- candlelight

Casting Instructions for the New House's Property Locator Magic

- Gather your supplies, clean the area where the spell will be performed, and prepare your map and pendulum.
- • Turn down the lights, light a few candles, and unwind.
- You should rub a little rosemary oil on your pendulum and ask it to tell you the best location for your new home while

massaging it clockwise.
- Lay the map face down on a flat surface like a table.
- Suspend the pendulum over the center of the map and allow it to swing in that direction freely.
- Cover your eyes with your hands and murmur to Pendulum, "Pendulum, I need you to work your magic for me. Please help me pick the best place for my future home." Let it therefore be.
- Please keep your hands quite still and open your eyes. You can anticipate your pendulum to begin swinging, whirling, or pulling in a particular way.
- Slowly move your hand in the pendulum's pulling direction in a circular motion.
- Request that the pendulum halt over the area where the inquiry is posed.
- Recording the location, thanking the pendulum and the map, and casting the final spell,

The dream home charm is the second of the new house spells.

Do you ever have fantasies about moving into a brand-new house? The ideal location to start a family and call home for you and your loved ones. On the other side, you probably don't know where to hunt for a house or how to get the required money. Check out our straightforward yet effective new home dream magic and discover how it performs for you.

You'll need the following to finish this project:

- A tiny house decoration or a playhouse in miniature.
- A fireplace or candle (if you are going to use a candle, you will also need a fireproof container, a bucket of water, or an extinguisher)
- You have some paper and a pencil in your possession.
- Sunflower or jojoba seed oil (vegetable or olive oil will suffice if you don't have any other options!).
- Lavender, catnip, marjoram, or saint john's wort are all thought to increase happiness.
- Just a tiny bit of any of these herbs—basil, nutmeg, oak bark—will boost your success.
- A small amount of rosemary, mint, nettle, or safe can be used as protection against injury.

Building Directions for the New House Spell:

- Gather all of your materials. Get the environment in your sacred space just right by turning down the light.
- Cleanse your environment, your supplies, and your body.
- Write anything down, and I'll have it straight away, or draw a picture of your ideal home. Be precise. Draw your dream house on paper and see yourself living there.
- Once you've done that, fold the paper once in your direction and sprinkle a pinch of each of the three herbs into the fold. Continue until the paper can be folded as small as possible. Continue folding it in your direction until there is as little paper left as the herbs are tucked inside.
- After that, safely burn your piece of paper to release your wish for your ideal home and send it into space. Imagine yourself simultaneously in your dream home, where you are happy, prosperous, and secure.
- Put a spoonful of oil in another basin and add the paper once it has been reduced to ash. Mix it thoroughly.
- While massaging the little dollhouse/dreamhouse with ash oil in a clockwise motion, repeat the following mantra: "Bring us a pleasant, protected, and successful dream home."
- The residual oil and ash should be kept in an airtight container.
- If you put your dream home decor on display in your current residence, it will be easier to keep seeing yourself living there until it happens. Every Friday, use the ash oil to anoint the new

house where you'll perform your dream magic.
- Then, before adding any further decorations to your new home, hang the toy replica of your perfect home from the rafters or the front porch as soon as you move in.

CAST STRONG SPELLS WITH THE JAR

Jar spells have just ascended to the top of the witchy popularity rankings, and it seems that they are just as common as bath rituals and crystal magick. My two-part hypothesis is that they are both simple to build and, when done effectively, highly impactful.

They may have their roots in American folk magic, at least in part, but they also resemble the old witch bottles used in Europe.

Throughout the United States and the British Isles, objects that resemble witch bottles have been discovered hidden in the ground, in the foundations of homes, and beneath fireplaces.

A witch bottle is simply a protection charm contained in a bottle. And, in my opinion, it is not restricted by any particular culture. At the very least, this particular form of witchcraft dates back to the early modern era.

Making your own magic jars is not against any laws, but you should be aware that it is not necessary to do so if you wish to avoid adhering to foreign cultural practices. Undoubtedly, some jar spells or "workings." come from the Hoodoo folk magic tradition. especially the jars used for "sweetening" honey and "souring" vinegar.

A jar spell is not only a collection of little components; it is a bottled spell that requires significant preparation and many moving pieces. Let's get started by figuring out how to cast your jar spell. But first, let's define a witch bottle.

What is a witch bottle?

Although witch bottles are one of the earliest forms of magic used in Britain, different kinds of bottle or jar spells have been discovered worldwide. In Britain, witch bottles were one of the first forms of magic.

Three factors contribute to the potency and popularity of the witch bottle, also known as the jar spell, their attractiveness, the countless ways in which they may be utilized, and the ease with which they can be produced.

"Jar Spells " is more accurate when referring to non-traditional witch bottles.

The first recorded use of the witch bottle occurred in the late Middle Ages or the early Renaissance. It was not created by witches but rather by regular people who desired to shield themselves from witches' influence. You'll discover that a significant portion of the traditional behaviors that are referred to as "witchcraft" are really a range of defensive mechanisms against the impact of witchcraft. The traditional ones usually had "piss and pins." as their two main parts. It was believed that the bottle would capture any negative energy that a witch could throw your way before returning it to her in the form of searing bladder pains. You would immediately hurry to the Witch to ask for assistance.

It is standard practice in traditional forms of witchcraft to use a person's urine for several purposes, one of which is because humans are animals, too; therefore, using one's pee in a protection spell is, quite literally, marking one's territory with it.

However, if you do not like to do so, you are not required to use your pee. Many new recipes are out there that call for crystals and herbs.

Why would you want to make a modern witch bottle?

The modern witch bottle is a simple and versatile method for casting spells; the question is, when should you use it? You should use them for spells that you will want to cast endlessly or for a long period, such as a protection bottle, or for situations in which you anticipate that the consequences may take some time to manifest, such as a new love spell if you are extremely selective.

Consider placing the magic inside of a tangible thing to protect it. The most effective uses for witch bottles, also known as magic jars, are those with an aura of protection. Where else do we treat objects (or people) in such a manner?

To prevent our money from being misplaced or taken, we store it in various containers, ranging from wallets to tins to piggy banks.

At night, we provide more security for ourselves and our families by securing the doors and windows.

We place priceless photographs and other happy mementos in albums to protect them from being lost or damaged.

To keep loved ones close at hand and secure, many wear lockets containing their hair or photographs of the people they cherish.

Ask yourself if you want to guard something before deciding whether a spell jar is an appropriate container for this particular conjuration. Spell jars are excellent for casting spells, including money, romance, friendships, protection, and defensive magic.

Make a witch bottle with a powerful spell by combining various kinds of alcohol with a chant. I get such a kick out of bringing together all of the different energies and then seeing the jar do its thing over the next few months. They are most effective when spells are deeply ingrained in the enchanted items.

Jars for spell casting

A witch's "bottle" is not required to be an antique bottle made of Glass. It's feasible that it's a jar and for it to be constructed of plastic, Glass, ceramic, or even metal. You can use whatever you choose if it has a lid that can keep liquids in but not air.

There's a chance you don't have a bottle of bellarmine sitting around the house. However, you have your pick from a very large selection of different containers to use as your witch's bottle. Listed below are some ideas to consider:

- Jars of olives, pickles, mayonnaise, and red sauce that have seen better days (clean them out well and cleanse them first)
- Bottles for spices (preferably made of glass, but plastic can do if you don't have any other option)
- Jars made of mason glass, fitted with airtight lids
- Bottles made of glass for olive oil and vinegar (you can purchase these at your local dollar store even)

- Ornate blue glass bottles, which I could purchase for a low price at various thrift stores.
- Jars and containers made of plastic.

There are several factors why we believe the glass is superior for producing witch's bottles. If you intend to bury it, you will not be polluting the planet with plastic, which takes an eternity to break down. If you bury it, you will not be doing this. If ever. However, if you only have plastic and your spell is extremely important, you should utilize plastic. Keep track of where you put the plastic bottle, and if you find that you can retrieve it later, do so.

Before using your jars or bottles, clean them thoroughly and ensure they are completely dry. It is essential to dry the ingredients, as mold can grow on some dried ingredients if they come into contact with even trace amounts of moisture. Take off any labels that can be removed, but don't worry too much about any logos or language that you won't be able to change. Just make sure that you take into consideration what each of these items is.

I wouldn't construct a jar for sobriety out of my jars with grapes on them, nor would I make a jar for world peace out of a glass of Pepsi.

When selecting a vessel for a particular spell, this is one of those areas in which you need to consider the beliefs that are unique to you as an individual.

One of the most potent ways to cast a protection spell on oneself is to create a witch bottle and bury it on one's property. This is an effective way of doing so. I strongly advise you to do so. In addition, they can be crafted for different uses and then placed strategically throughout the home to bring magic to you. Make a love potion as a bottle and store it in your bedroom. The potion should contain love herbs as well as other personal items. If you need healing or money, you can make witch bottles using the relevant materials and store them in your home in a location that is connected to your purpose.

Witch bottles: all you need to know

Witches and those who desired to protect themselves from witches have used witch bottles for hundreds of years. Historically, they were employed to shield the individual from the effects of black magic and bad spirits. People use them for various purposes, including love, protection, and healing.

The archaeological evidence we have for witch bottles makes them one of the most important artifacts in the history of witchcraft. Jars and vessels made of clay and glass dating back hundreds of years have been discovered in England and the United States. These archaeological relics are classified by historians based on the items that they include, such as pins, needles, nails, broken glass, wood, cloth, personal human effects (such as fingernail clippings, hair, bone, urine, and so on), and occasionally herbs or stones.

Bottles used in witchcraft are generally buried in the ground close to the entrance of a home or elsewhere on the property. Sometimes the bottle would be buried beneath the hearth so that the heat might "light up" the contents.

The use of witch bottles for protection and healing dates back millennia.

A genuine witch bottle from the Bellarmine brand

Witch bottles are one kind of archeological evidence supporting the presence of witches.

A well-known witch bottle that was recently discovered in London during an archaeological study is known as the Holywell Witch Bottle. The witch bottle, which historians think belongs to the late seventeenth or early eighteenth century and was used during the Salem witch trials, included pins, nails, and maybe a piece of bone.

Curiously, the majority of witch bottles are from the 1600s, a time when there was a genuine dread of witches. However, the witch bottle was identified as being from the 1800s, and as a consequence, associations with the Witch of Saratoga have been formed. On the other hand, Tubbs was around during the whole seventeenth century. She was thus unable to have been the bottle's maker. This finding, however, demonstrates that this form of magic has been practiced for a long time.

Exhibit at the Witch House in Salem

Utilizations in witchcraft throughout the ages

There is a great deal of speculation over the exact purpose intended to be served by the witch bottle. This is because there was probably more than one application, like how witches now utilize them for various magical purposes.

Its Primary Purpose Is To Provide Protection FROM Witchcraft

One of a witch bottle's main purposes is protection, and it is a highly potent means of warding off evil spirits, curses, and black magic. Glass is usually used to make witch bottles. For the purpose we are discussing, the witch bottle is well-known to the majority of people. Why, in the first place, would someone need defense against curses and evil spirits?

People used to believe that witches were everywhere in the globe and were to blame for all bad things that happened, such as illness, accidents, a poor crop, adverse weather, and so on. Every time someone believed they were the target of a witch's vengeance, they had to take protective precautions. A witch's bottle was regularly used for this same reason.

Healing

Healing is also another application for witch bottles. In the past, whenever someone became ill or injured, people pointed the finger at supernatural forces as the cause.

Either they were thought to have transferred their illnesses into an item such as a witch bottle, or they were needed to eliminate a curse or an evil spirit in order to cure. In some parts of the southern USA, people practice a method of healing in which they transfer their ailment to an object, most commonly a tree or a stone. This is a type of magic known as contagion magic, sometimes known as transference, in which the energy from one person is transmitted into another thing.

In the interests of the house

Although it was formerly commonplace, nowadays there is no longer the custom of blessing a home before it is built. In the traditions of Eastern Europe and other parts of the globe, an offering consisting of a sacrifice would be put there for the spirits of the land in the hope that the spirits would bless the house being constructed and the people who would ultimately reside in it. According to one school of thinking, witch bottles were used in sacrificial rituals or as sacrifices to the faeries that guarded the dwellings or the land.

How exactly do witch bottles accomplish their goals?

We are aware of their value and strength, but how do they really work?

With the intention of attracting an evil spirit or witch to the person who is meant to be their victim, personal things from people, such as fingernail clippings, hair, a piece of clothing, and body fluids, are put in witch bottles, according to a modern witch.

If you bury the bottle holding the witch bottle, the spirit within will be "grounded" or placed to rest by the soil itself. Once the spirit has entered the bottle, the pins, nails, and other sharp objects within the container "stick" or trap it, preventing it from exiting the container again. The ghost is tricked into believing that the departed individual is kept within the bottle.

Using to Banish or Release

Make witch bottles to release something from your life or to exorcise it, then dispose of them far away from your home and yourself. Throw it into flowing water, bury it near a busy crossroads, or dispose of it in the landfill as far away as you can! You shouldn't put a sickness in a witch bottle and bury it on your property since doing so can bring the illness back. Why? If it's still in the area, it hasn't been eradicated.

Because evil spirits can be focusing on you and your property, this is not the same as a typical bottle for protection. However, you may draw their attention away from you and your house if you bury a witch bottle on your land.

Spell jars

Jars referred to as "spell jars." are used in the practice of witchcraft, which involves the casting of spells and the performance of rituals. Old mason jars or repurposed jam jars are often utilized for their construction. Once constructed, the jars are carefully loaded with a variety of herbs, plants, oils, crystals, and salts in order to assist in the materialization of a particular objective. During the process of conjuring their jar, witches would repeat their objectives or participate in mental rehearsals in order to elevate it to the level of a religious ritual.

When they are done, spell jars are exhibited in a prominent position to serve as a wonderful reminder of what the person is attempting to bring into their lives and serve as a fantastic reminder of what the person is trying to bring into their lives.

Instructions for making a jar spells

There are several different recipes for magic jars that have been given for you below; choose the one that you want to create first. After that, gather together all of the components that are required for the ritual, and choose a time and location for it to take place. It is possible that doing it on a new moon or a full moon will be effective, or even on one of the other sabbats of the Wheel, such as Ostara, Samhain, or Yule, if it is a part of a new intention for that season. However, this is only the case if you are performing the ritual in conjunction with a new intention for that season.

Before you get started, you may want to try meditation to help you become centered and into a positive frame of mind. Make sure you're in a place that's soothing and pleasant so you can rest there. If you like having music in the background, you may want to play some. You may want to try burning some incense, garden sage, rosemary, lavender, or palo santo at your site in order to get rid of any lingering odors or impurities in the air.

Place all of the contents into the jar, and then rearrange them as necessary until you are pleased with the way it appears. When you are finished putting the lid on your jar of spells, don't forget to state your purpose out loud! Your jar has to be sealed with the candle wax that stands for your objective (e.g., use a pink candle when making a self-love spell jar).

Take joy in fashioning something exquisite out of the myriad of natural components that the earth provides. You may find it useful to say a brief prayer, repeat a few affirmations, or image yourself living the life of your dreams as if it were already happening. You might also try visualizing yourself living the life of your dreams as if it were already happening.

When you are completed, record your recipe in your spellbook (if you don't already have one, make one now!) and keep a record of how well your spell jar has functioned over the course of time. It will be beneficial to return back to this and use it as a reference when seeking to build another one of these in the future.

Keep in mind that the recipes for the spell jars that have been supplied for you here are just designed to act as a guide for you. You are not have to follow them to the letter, especially when considering the fact that there are a lot of different plants and stones that indicate similar things. Don't be in such a rush to get out and purchase a number of different things. To begin, you should focus on making the most of what you currently own. When it comes to making magic jars, the energy and intention that you put into them is the single most crucial factor. Put objects in your spell jar that you have a deep affection for and that have a particular place in your heart. Put your trust in your innate sense of right and wrong.

Ingredients & tools you might require

- Incense made from the herbs of your choice to be burned.
- Mason jars or upcycled jam jars (any jar will do)
- Essential oils
- Various salts (e.g., sea salt, Himalayan salt, rock salt, black salt)
- Herbs and spices, either fresh or dried
- Plants and flowers gathered from the wild (flowers and dry petals can be used too)

- Honey
- Crystals
- Candles of many hues and hue combinations
- a lighter or a box of matches
- A pen
- Your diary or other books of spells

USING YOUR SPELL JARS

Where would you recommend i put it?

I'll go into detail on where you should keep the various spell jars and their corresponding recipes in a bit.

One potent technique to boost the efficacy of a self-love spell is to place the jar with the spell in front of a mirror as a daily reminder of the love you intend to offer yourself.

But generally speaking, you may put your spell jars anywhere you choose! In your home office, beside the front entrance, on your witchcraft altar, or just next to your bed. Whenever and whenever suits you most.

Advice on lighting candles

For certain spells, a witch would burn a candle over a sealed jar of wax and let it burn down to nothing. Repeat this procedure until the candle is entirely snuffed out. Since there is a possibility of it catching fire, you should dispose of it in the sink.

How long will the magic in my jar keep working?

However, there are no rules that must be strictly adhered to while doing your ritual or establishing how long your spell jar must be kept after usage. Keep it until your goals are realized or until the contents start to seem a bit dry and lifeless and need to be changed, whichever comes first. Possibly both of those things might happen. Donating organic materials to the soil, including seeds and plants, is essential.

Don't forget to clean your gear before use!

You should remember to wash and refresh any crystals you utilize in your spell jars. To do this, put the items in a bowl of water and set it on a windowsill during a full moon.

Notes this when making your spell jars

1. **USE YOUR IMAGINATION AND LISTEN TO YOUR GUT INSTINCTS.**

There is no such thing as doing anything in the incorrect manner when it comes to the process of building a spell jar. You can find a way to put them to use in nearly any circumstance thanks to the almost infinite number of applications. Make use of this list as a starting point and a point of reference, but don't let it limit you to using just the components that are mentioned here. There are literally hundreds of different kinds of plants, herbs, oils, and crystals, and each one of them could have a distinct significance. When choosing your elements, it is of the utmost importance that they, in your opinion, adequately reflect whatever it is that you are striving to accomplish.

2. **MEDITATE ON & ENVISION YOUR INTENTIONS**

Consistently working with your spell jar will assist to enhance the amount of energy that is contained inside it. Sit in front of what it is that you want to think about, or take it in your hands and concentrate on it as you think about it. Imagine for a moment that this spell is working as intended and producing the expected results.

3. **BE DELIBERATE IN YOUR ACTIONS.**

Check to see if you are also carrying out the action in the world that already exists. For instance, if you want to attract a happy, loving relationship, you need to make sure that you are putting the effort in to meet new people both online and in real life. You may meet people in real life by going out and talking to them, or you can meet people online by talking to them. You might accomplish your goal by going on dates or by attending activities. If you want your business to be even more successful, you need to make sure that you put in the effort to find new customers or consumers that are interested in the items or services that you provide.

4. **HAVE FAITH IN THE MAGIC CONTAINED IN YOUR SPELL JAR.**

Because faith is one of the main building blocks of witchcraft and magic, it is necessary for you to have faith in the rites and spells that you carry out in order to be successful. Believe in the magic that may be found not just in yourself but also in the world around you and the cosmos. Believe without a doubt that the universe is on your side and that it wants to assist you in reaching your ambitions just as much as you want it to. Have confidence that this is the case.

The crucial elements that make up a jar spell

So, what exactly do you need to perform a jar spell? A jar equipped with a lid. However, you will also require components that correspond to your goals. After making a good number of spell jars, I've discovered that the most effective components are dry and non-perishable. If you put fresh ingredients in your jar, you'll have to deal with problems caused by mold. Mold can also be caused by plant matter that hasn't been entirely dried up. I can guarantee you that it will start to smell bad there.

Therefore, select ingredients such as the ones listed below.

- A jar that has a cover for it (obviously)
- Dried Lavender, rosemary, thyme, mugwort, chamomile, mint, roses, cinnamon, and other herbs can be found in your spice cupboard or herb cabinet.
- Make sure the flowers and flower petals are dehydrated before using them.
- Either the common table salt in your kitchen cabinet or some witch's black salt. Protection and purification rituals make effective use of salt's potent properties.
- Sugar is an excellent component for use in love and money pots
- Effective in money jars are both coins and bills in dollar denominations.
- When it comes to stones and crystals, it's better to break them up into tiny pieces. This is true if you want to shake the jar once it's filled (large chunks might easily break it!).
- Items from the natural world, such as feathers, acorns, and

other things.
- Sand is utilized in ocean spells, fertility spells, and abundance spells.
- Using pins and needles in protection jars, comparable to the old Witch's bottles, is very beneficial.
- Intentions written down on paper: take a piece of paper, write down your goal, and place it in the jar.
- Roots, nuts, bark
- Dirt or soil: originating from a variety of locations that provide fuel for your aim (a pinch is best)

Anything you believe contributes to your goal can fit in the jar!

The key to successfully casting your spell with a jar!

Put all ingredients in the jar, screw on the lid, and shake it well. You're done. Right? WRONG. In a nutshell, the steps are comprised of that, which is to say, yes. However, your jar magic will likely fail if you don't put effort into the process and don't give it any thought. Mindlessly performing any ritual will have few to no results. I am speaking from personal experience.

An infinite number of ghosts can be called upon to aid in casting a spell. Spirits from plants, animals, and stones are the most commonly used. When working on your intention, you may already have a god or other supernatural being in mind. Hekate, in her role as Queen of the Witches, is, in any case, constantly involved.

You may also research to determine which god or being is most compatible with you and this specific endeavor. The more you are familiar with the spirits being called upon; the more effective the magic will be. These magical entities have a wide variety of intricate properties and personalities that are all their own.

> Keep reading for further in-depth explanations.

> **Jar Spells 101:**
> - A jar spell is a spell purposefully placed in a jar with a lid
> - Jar spells are made for many intentions: love, protection, money, healing and more
> - Correspond your ingredients with your intentions
> - Be careful of the ingredients you put in the jar: some household products can chemically react (i.e. vinegar and eggshells will foam up)
> - Best ingredients for jar spells include: salt, herbs, stones, coins, pendants, and your written spell on a piece of paper
> - Seal it and shake it and/or burn a candle on top

Define your intent

Establishing your purpose is the most important stage in performing a spell involving a jar. Your intention is the pivot point around which your spell will revolve. The intention of the spell might be thought of as its "mission statement." Crisp, clear, and concisely stated. Brief sentences. Strong verbs. An effective method for separating the meaning from the words used is to use a word web.

As is customary when working with magic, your goal should be to:

SPECIFIC: Concentrate on specific objectives.

REALISTIC: Check to see if those objectives can be achieved (no Dungeons & Dragons or Harry Potter fantasy stuff).

ETHICAL: I'm not going to tell you what is or isn't ethical, but you should give some thought to your spiritual ethics and examine how your actions may affect others and the world around you.

After deciding what you want to accomplish, you can proceed to the following stage of creating your jar spell, deciding what items to place within the jar.

Take, for instance:

A protection spell covers many topics, from driving away your enemies to ensuring that your health remains in good shape. The growth is not a wild roller coaster ride of ups and downs but rather steady and sustainable. Additionally, you will desire success, which may involve contributing something to the world that is useful to you and the larger community.

Select a vessel for your jar spell.

For the most part, a spell can be cast using virtually any container. Using containers made of plastic does not make me feel completely at ease; nonetheless, opinions on how successful it differs. Glass is my material of choice, although clay and other things are also used. You are clear as long as there are no cracks in the container and the top or cork fits securely.

Look around the house and in second-hand stores for a bottle that will do the job. You may use everything from mason jars and baby food jars to jars for mayonnaise or pickles and vintage bottles for salad dressing and olive oil.

Note: Before you begin, ensure that the container you intend to use and all the materials you intend to place inside have been purified and consecrated.

Paint your jar (optional)

You can paint your jar with images, symbols, and colors that coincide with your purpose. This is not required, but any assistance might give you a lift, no matter how small. In addition, it prevents the contents of your jar from being seen by anyone who might witness it.

The appropriate components in play

Check to see whether you have all of the necessary components. Ingredients that align with and feed your goal, as well as those that won't undergo any chemical reactions or exploratory processes in the jar while you're sleeping. Pick a jar that is solidly built and comes with a lid for use in your project. If you can manage it, make sure the container is airtight! Jars that have been used in the past and are now being recycled are still another excellent choice. Ensure that they are pristine, and then perform a spiritual cleansing on them, before putting them to use.

You have a lot of different alternatives to choose from while you're filling up your jar, so take your time making your decision.

The decision-making process of what will be included into this miraculous operation is the most crucial aspect of the process. Even if there is no limitation on what you may add, it is very important that you choose items that will help you make progress toward the ultimate magical goal that you have set for yourself. In spite of this, there is no restriction on what you may put in your submission. You are required to check that each item has been "charged." before putting anything into your jar.

Timing

Your next consideration should be the appropriate time for the jar spell you want to cast. If you wish to cast a spell with the assistance of magical timing, you need do some study to determine the ideal day and planetary hour to cast the spell so that it has the most possible impact.

Think about using the many phases of the moon as an illustration. Jar spells should be casted during the waxing phase of the moon in order to achieve personal and spiritual growth, increased beauty, the attraction of love and friendship, a boost to your money account, and other objectives of a similar kind. At the time of the full moon, swift and powerful manifestation might take place. The crescent moon in its declining phase is a metaphor for casting out, binding, and getting rid of things or people who aren't desired. Altering the timeframe of a spell may also be accomplished by changing the day of the week, the hour, or the time of day, amongst other variables. If you want to disregard the temporal component, you are allowed to do so; but, doing so may lead your spell to be less effective. The presence of favorable conditions almost always results in favorable outcomes.

Filling your jar

After you have prepared yourself by being focused and grounded, you should start by taking up one object at a time in order to charge it (or by placing it on your pentacle). When you charge anything, you infuse it with the power of your goal while also simultaneously stirring up and stimulating the thing's underlying natural energy, which you are aiming to draw from.

It is time to create an incantation that will ignite all of your energy if you have chosen to seek aid from spirits. If you have made this decision, now is the time to do so. The invocation acts as a leader for the spirits that have been summoned to assist in the spell's execution. Incantations may be made up of utterances, actions, and emotions all at the same time. If more energy is put in the direction that is being provided, there is a greater chance that the spirit will follow out the instructions that are being given to it.

After the spirits have been chosen (or have presented themselves on their own), the chant should be designed such that each spirit is explicitly summoned. This should be done so that the spirits may be called upon as needed. In addition to that, be sure to include sections in which you elaborate on your main goal. I will teach you the magic that I have used for my own success, development, and defense throughout my life.

It is important to keep in mind that you do not need to draw a circle in order to cast this spell; however, if you would want to do it inside a ceremonial circle, you are more than welcome to do so.

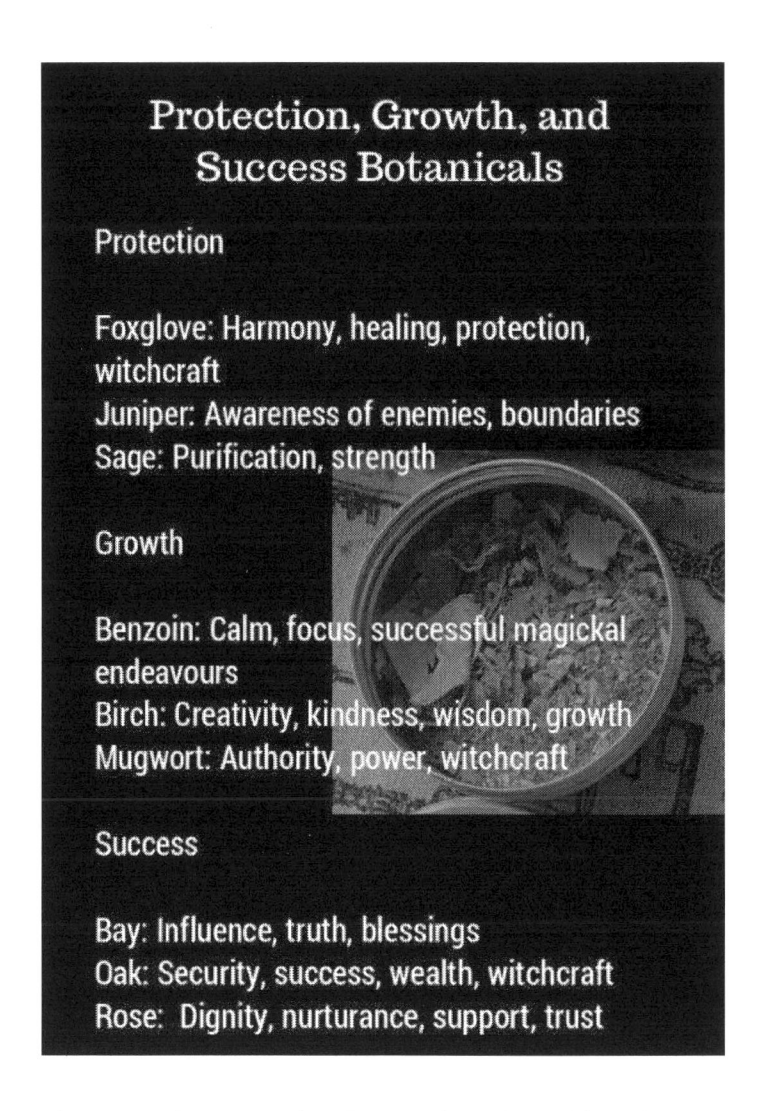

> ## Protection, Growth, and Success Botanicals
>
> **Protection**
>
> Foxglove: Harmony, healing, protection, witchcraft
> Juniper: Awareness of enemies, boundaries
> Sage: Purification, strength
>
> **Growth**
>
> Benzoin: Calm, focus, successful magickal endeavours
> Birch: Creativity, kindness, wisdom, growth
> Mugwort: Authority, power, witchcraft
>
> **Success**
>
> Bay: Influence, truth, blessings
> Oak: Security, success, wealth, witchcraft
> Rose: Dignity, nurturance, support, trust

You can increase the strength of your chant by adding items to your jar. For instance, while you are filling your jar with rose quartz, you could say something like, "I charge you, rose quartz, to draw love to me with the graces of the Goddess Aphrodite through the power of

Earth, Air, Fire, and Water; with the power of the sun, moon, and stars." This would be a good way to charge the rose quartz to bring love to you.

The power of words

When I am ready to cast a spell, I always figure out a chant that I will recite. Increasing your energy level is a wonderful benefit of chanting. You can discover a chant in a book or look it up on the internet; alternatively, you can come up with your own. Effective communication does not require the use of Shakespeare. Something straightforward will do just fine, for example:

- I want money, money, bring it to me;
- Please assist me in paying these expenses that I notice.

It will be successful if it is appropriate for the event and has personal significance for you.

Make an effort to construct magic with rhyming verses, as this will allow you to harness the power of the rhythm and the strength of the words. My rhymes will never be able to take first place in a poetry slam, but they do the job. When creating your chants, employing a comfortable and natural framework is important. Your spirits will question your sincerity if you cannot recite the incantation with the necessary level of authority and self-assurance.

Incantation activities include the procedures employed with correspondences and spirits, such as combining botanicals precisely. Other examples of these approaches include the usage of spirits. Invoking the feelings connected to accomplishing your objective is another beneficial strategy. Faking it till you make it.

The most general spirit should be invoked first, followed by the more specific ones, and finally, expressions of appreciation and release should be offered to the spirits.

If you prefer this method, rhythm and rhyme can also help you learn it fast before you begin, and once you have it down, you can get into it and use it as a mantra while you're casting. By allowing it to flow easily from your lips, you are allowing it to bypass the conscious part of your brain and tap into your source of power, which is the part of the mind that directs the energy toward achieving your objective.

Casting

The most exciting step comes: merging the incantation, correspondences, and spirits you have selected into a powerful spell.

If there is conflict, disarray, or distress in the area in which you will be completing the task, you might need to cleanse the area first, and you might also need to cast a circle. This will depend on the atmosphere in which you cast the spell. During the casting process, a black candle is an excellent aid for warding off any potential interlopers.

Casting with awareness

Put in your all into creating your jar by devoting your whole being to the process, including your head, your heart, and your body. Don't just go through the motions of the steps. Really think about what you're doing. You should do everything you need to in order to effectively focus on what it is that you want to achieve. Make the necessary adjustments to your environment and train your mind to be open, calm, and focused. You should practice visualizing it, singing it, and verbalizing it out loud. Those are your three options. As you place each component into the jar, be sure to explain its purpose to yourself and others out loud. After you have checked the container to ensure that everything is there, replace the lid on the jar.

Casting a spell on your jar

The next step, which many would argue is the most important, is to FEED your spell jar. Increase the amount of your energy that it has to operate with. You will be successful in achieving this objective if you shake your jar while simultaneously whispering your goals into it or praying over it. You might also try lighting a candle and putting it in the jar before covering it with the lid. Choose a certain number of days to have candles burning on the top, and coordinate the times at which the candles are lit with the suitable times for performing the spell (as mentioned above in the section on timing).

For instance, if you want to attract a new love interest, light a candle in your jar for a period of six days. A completely new creative project is allowed time for throughout the course of three days. Holding the magic jar in your hands as you talk about your aspirations and objectives is a bare minimum need.

Put the lid on your jar.

You can immediately shut the bottle once you have completed filling the jar. There is no cause for concern that the spell won't be able to break free of the jar because the spirits contained within can move freely through both space and time.

Putting wax caps on the jars.

You are not obliged to use wax to seal your jars, and if there is even a distant possibility that you may want to disassemble your jar in the following few weeks, I would suggest you not to use wax since it will make it more difficult for you to do so. If wax seals are broken, the wax will spread EVERYWHERE after it has been released. Since of this, using wax sealing is an excellent choice to make if you want your bottle to endure for a long time because it ensures that the magic will remain the same throughout the duration of its usage.

You will need a candle, a flame, and a dish that can tolerate heat in order to heat the jar properly. The jar should be placed in the heat-resistant dish while it is being heated. When you do this, you need to be really careful since you might burn yourself on the hot wax. Burning a candle on top of the lid, around the lid, or in the open mouth of the jar is one way to hermetically seal the jar.

Please take note that candles are not required for jar spells.

However, I have discovered that combining it with candle magic results in an additional increase in strength. If you want to use a candle in your jar, locate one of the suitable colors and dress it. Then, start the candle inside the jar's mouth or on top of the tightly closed jar., allowing all of the wax to melt down as it burns. You can keep a continuing flame on top of a jar that holds many candles for a project that will go on for some time.

Meditate on your intention while charging the bottle.

Imagine that you've already accomplished what you set out to do. Instead of visualizing yourself as someone who wants your objective, picture yourself as someone who already has it. This will prevent you from getting stuck in a cycle of desiring. When everything is said and done, what will your life be like, and how will you feel?

Maintain your focus on the image for at least twenty minutes or as long as possible.

Charging

There are primarily two approaches to establishing an aim while working with these spells. You can either utter the words out loud or think them to yourself to set your purpose. Between the two possibilities, there is no obvious winner. You may be more drawn to one of them than the other, and that's where the answer lies.

If you want to say something, you can make it as simple or elaborate as you would like. Later on, each verbal and written form of spellcasting will be covered in its separate modules.

Something like "I intend for you to use this bottle for..." I satiate you with (ingredient) and continue (ingredient). Make it so (the intention) works out for me.

What should you do with your spell jar after casting your spell?

When the process of casting your spell has been completed, you will be given the opportunity to choose what to do with the jar.

After you have done performing the spell on the jar, you will have a number of options available to you. You may either demolish it, bury it, conceal it, toss it in water, or keep it on your altar as an offering. These are the effectively your five choices. Which path you choose to pursue is dependent on the objectives that you have established for yourself in the future.

If you want to bury your bottle in the ground, the only thing you can do with it after that is leave it where you plan to bury it. There is nothing more you can do with it. But if you wish to keep the bottle, when the spell's effects have worn off, you should take a look around your home or place of work; you could find yourself wondering what to do with it. It is totally dependent on the activities in which you feel the most at ease.

However, we cannot stress enough how important it is to get rid of any bottles or jars that were used in the casting of harmful spells. You should get rid of the bottle by either tossing it away or disposing of it in a very remote area if, for example, you are using it to drive away a disease or a person. In this case, you should get rid of the bottle.

Nevertheless, whether it was used to attract money, friendship, love, or anything else, you should bury it in the easternmost section of your property. This is the best location for it. This makes it possible for the sun to rise on the results, which in turn provides them with a steady supply of energizing and encouraging energy. OR you might bury it towards the west, so that the findings would be illuminated by the sun as it was setting. In other words, we have completed it.

If any of the following apply:

You are seeking for a solution to either permanently protect yourself from a curse or break the curse that has been placed on you. If you do not have access to your property, you may bury it in a flower pot that is filled with dirt and put it on your front porch. If you do not have access to your land, you can bury it in a flower pot. This will protect your property and allow you to keep a watchful look out for potential invaders.

You want your jar to have the effect of a "magnet" that continuously draws things to you so that you may gather them all (attention, health, wealth, etc.). Put a stop to it once and for all. You may cast for it by burying it on your property or on the property of the person you're looking for.

You are working on curing yourself (or the person you are casting for) of something, such as an illness or an unwanted habit like as smoking or drinking too much. Alternatively, you are working on curing the person you are casting for. Bury the jar in the center of a busy intersection, don't look back, and (if at all possible) don't come back.

You have performed a spell on the target without their knowledge, but you must not lose sight of your morals in the process! Bury it on their property; preferably, you should do it in a location where they will see it on a regular basis, such as under their front door.

If any of the following apply:

I know it is difficult to bury a jar when living in an apartment. You desire to bury it but cannot since it is not an option. If this is the case, you should conceal it somewhere deep within the house, such as inside a wall, in the storage cupboard for old things, or in any other location where it won't be disturbed.

You plan to take it apart sometime in the future, which, if done correctly, will cause the spell to be rendered ineffective.

Place the jar of water if any of the following apply: *

You can use it to drive away or exorcise any creatures. You should also do it if you are interacting with beings that could be considered "questionable." It will be cleansed by the natural water sources running, protecting you from their subsequent visit.

The alternative to burying it at a crossroads is this. It has effectively removed a curse, a disease, a bad habit, and other similar issues. It is important to remember that you may be subject to a fine for littering if you throw things into the local waters.

***Tip:** If it tends to float, you should tie a weight to it or make a hole in the cap.

Keep the jar on your altar if any of the following apply:

You'd like to continue working toward your ongoing goal. To keep it working for you, you can either keep lighting candles and placing them over the jar's opening or shake the jar while reciting the chant.

You can also keep it in a shrine to your god or goddess if you have petitioned them for assistance and built one. Again, you can keep the power going by shaking it every once in a while while you chant.

This is an excellent option for spells that will demand a lot of time and work; for instance, if you were to make a jar spell to assist you in passing tests, you might keep it on your altar through college. This is a good option for spells requiring much time and effort. Spells that require a great deal of time and effort have this as an option. The night before your examinations, you may try shaking it, shaking out your chant, or burning a candle. It is preferable to do this rather than create a new spell for each examination.

If any of the following apply:

You no longer require the spell's strength and would prefer the effects to cease immediately. For instance, if you used a jar charm to bring love into your life, you might have been interested in many other things for a period. Because you are about to get married, you do not wish to pique the interest of any other potential suitors. Therefore, you would put an end to the enchantment.

To accomplish this, empty the container into running water or bury the contents somewhere else, then clean the container thoroughly before throwing it away. It is feasible to reuse it if the necessary cleaning procedures are carried out first.

Caution: Unless you are very familiar with what you are doing, it is not a good idea to deconstruct a jar used for cursing, hexing, or breaking a curse or hex. Put it in moving water or bury it at a busy intersection, and you'll have nothing more to worry about.

Do Not Set Fire to Your Sacred Jar!

It is suggested in some sources that you should throw it into a fire. However, this is an approach you should avoid using. In particular, this was a way to cast curses and break curses. The Witch would toss the jar into the fire, and if it shattered, it signaled either that the curse was effective (causing the person it was placed on to suffer) or that the curse you were removing had been lifted.

This is not required at all and is not a secure choice. However, if you disassemble jar magic and have some components left over (ribbon, paper, etc.), you could burn those objects after it's demolished if you have a safe method. This would apply only if you dismantled the spell and had some components left over.

Should You Put A Bottle Or Jar Back Into Use Once A Spell Has Been Completed?

Glass bottles and jars are frequently used and recycled by witches once the spells have been executed successfully. Unless you've used it to get rid of anything or to banish something, we don't see anything improper with this practice. In this particular scenario, getting rid of it is most likely to be the best course of action. However, if you would like to reuse a bottle or jar that was used successfully, you should thoroughly clean it and spiritually purify it before using it again.

Fire can heat witch bottles, which enables the bottles to be sealed after they have been heated.

How to get rid of the remains of the spell jar

Once the spell's effects have taken place, what should you do with the jar? It does depend on what your intentions are. I figure out how to get rid of the remaining contents of my spell jar by applying logic to the problem.

For instance, if I put a spell on a money jar and the money starts rolling in. Still, I don't want the money to cease coming in, and I will normally bury the remnants of the money jar at the easternmost part of my property. I remove the lid from the jar and tip the contents onto the ground. You are free to bury the entire jar if you choose; however, if you have a tiny yard and are simply placing a ton of Glass and metal into the ground, you will eventually run out of space.

Having said that, if you created a spell jar for more "gray" purposes, you should avoid opening it. To add insult to injury, you shouldn't bury it anyplace close to you. I would throw the full jar away (without opening it) at a remote location.

Bury the remains of the jar spell in the westernmost part of your property if you get the impression that the spell wasn't successful and you want to begin the process all over again. After that, give the jar and lid a thorough cleaning so that you can reuse them if you choose.

Burial of jar spells

Be sure that the components of the spell and the container it contains are biodegradable materials if you intend to bury it. Any spell that taints or pollutes the Earth, as well as the numerous Spirits involved with the land, is not likely to be looked upon favorably by the Earth. Glass should be avoided in particular. Containers made of Glass or ceramic can shatter when subjected to the pressure of the Earth. When these shards come to the surface, they pose a risk of injury to anyone or any animal that happens to step on them, unaware that they are there.

Accepting responsibility for one's deeds is required to fulfill the role of a witch. Find a container appropriate for burying your spells, or devise an alternative. Many witch bottles can be used as charming decorations, but if you'd rather not look at them, you can always put them in boxes or on the back of the shelf.

AUTHENTIC RECIPES FOR JAR SPELLS.

Spell jars, which are often referred to as witch bottles, have been crafted by practicing witches by hand for centuries, and these jars have been utilized by witches to bring about the most profound and emotional of their goals. And if you are a woman who has many various goals in mind for your life, you don't have to restrict yourself to just one spell jar; rather, you may create as many of them as you see fit!

If you are a baby witch who is just beginning out in witchcraft, spell jars are a terrific way to get your feet wet in the realm of witchcraft and a great way to start practicing true magic.

In addition, these jars would look beautiful placed anywhere in your house, or even on your desk at work, if you were to take them there. Remember that every woman has the ability to engage in witchcraft, so keep that in mind. A lady who is self-assured in her abilities and patterns her daily activities after the cycles of mother nature is all that is required to be considered a witch. You are not need to follow any one religion or engage in repeated rituals, and you most definitely do not need to use a broomstick. Neither of these things are required.

Crafting these spell jars is a fantastic hobby for hearth witches, particularly to engage in since they are so enthusiastic about anything creative and crafts that may assist improve the appearance of their home.

I will present a number of different recipes that, when combined, may result in one, but the one I give you will depend on what it is that you want.

Let's get started!

Self-love spell jar

INGREDIENTS:

- Rose petals
- Lavender
- Pink Himalayan salt
- Lemon
- Sandalwood
- Crystals: rose quartz or transparent quartz
- A candle in a pink hue
- A scrap of paper on which you've written some of your favorite self-love quotes or affirmations

METHOD:

- Place everything in the jar in the order that you choose, and continue doing so until you are pleased with how it appears.
- Light your candle, and after it has completely burned down, use the melted pink wax to close the jar. •
- Place the jar with the self-love spell in a prominent area in your home, such as on your altar or dressing table, to serve as a continual reminder to do acts of self-love and self-care.

Love spell jar

INGREDIENTS:

- Rose petals of any color, including pink, red, or white, as well as thorns, honey
- A single slug of liquor
- Lavender
- Patchouli
- Basil
- Cinnamon
- A rose quartz crystal
- Rose oil
- A sheet of paper on which your goals are written.
- A crimson candle.

METHOD:

The focus of this love spell jar, in contrast to that of a self-love spell jar, is on the love that exists between two individuals rather than the love that exists inside a person. It is also known as a honey jar spell, and it is the perfect jar to employ if you want to attract more love and romance into your life, as well as bring you the right romantic companion to share it with. You may find it easier to get into the right frame of mind if you listen to sensuous or romantic music in the background. Create a clear objective for the future of your love partnership and write it down as if it has already been attained. If you want to make it more fascinating, you might write it with your favorite lipstick. After meticulously placing all of the components inside of the mason jar, you may next use the crimson candle wax to close the jar.

Love jar spell recipe

This jar of love spells is designed to entice the proper kind of partner to come into your life. By doing so, rather than trying to force a connection, you are giving the decision to locate your ideal partner over to the hands of chance or the cosmos.

YOU WILL REQUIRE THE FOLLOWING:

- A jar that has a cover for it.
- Love-attracting herbs (you choose three): Lavender, rose, hibiscus and jasmine are some choices
- One little crystal or stone capable of attracting love; some examples include jade and rose quartz
- 6 Drops of an Essential Oil that can arouse romantic feelings, such as rose, ylang-ylang, orange, or bergamot
- Use of a pen and paper

INSTRUCTIONS FOR MAKING YOUR LOVE JAR:

- Purge your love jar magic components using whichever cleansing method strikes your fancy.
- Establish the tone. Turn on the radio, turn on the lights, etc.
- On the piece of paper, jot down your goals and objectives. While I write my over and over again six times, you can approach this however you see fit.
- Rotate the paper so that it faces you. Put it into the glass jar.
- Before placing the crystal in the jar, you should first state your intention aloud over the crystal.
- I begin by pouring Lavender into the jar about a third of the way, followed by roses, and finishing with jasmine almost to the top of the container. After that, you should give each herb a quick blast of air before placing it in the container. Keep an image of the ideal partner in your mind while you go through this process.
- Then, drizzle your essential oil over the components contained in the jar while reciting the mantra: "by three times three, for the ultimate good of all, the appropriate romantic love shall freely come to me."
- Put the lid on the jar, and set it aside.
- Keep the jar in your hands as you recite the following love spell: "I'm ready for love. I am love. The one who is meant for me will find me. By the authority of the product of three and three. Therefore, let it be."

- On top of the jar, you should light a pink or red candle. NEVER LEAVE UNATTENDED Objects or Areas! SAFETY FIRST!

If you are looking for romantic love, I recommend leaving the jar in your bedroom while a candle is burned on top of it every day for six days.

<u>Happiness spell jar</u>

INGREDIENTS:

- Petals of several wildflowers
- Sweetgrass
- Dandelion
- Saffron
- Seeds or petals from a sunflower.
- Amazonite, sunstone, tiger eye, and citrine are examples of crystals.
- A picture or photograph that gives you pleasure.
- Anything else that brings a smile and reminds you of good times.
- A gold or yellow candle

METHOD:

Be very certain that each new thing you put into the jar provides you genuine happiness and that it does so every time you look at it. If you want to draw in good energy, you are going to need this joyful spell jar more than anything else. It is recommended that you light a candle of your choosing, and while you are doing so, you should make sure to remember to close the jar with some of the melted wax.

At a perfect world, the jars of happiness would be exhibited in a spot where the sun could shine on them.

Happy home spell jar

INGREDIENTS:

- Basil
- Thyme
- Catnip
- Lavender
- Lemon peel or lemon balm
- Vanilla bean or extract
- Crystals: citrine, rose quartz, or amazonite
- A yellow candle

METHOD:

- Gather all your components and place them in the jar while you think about the energy you want to permeate throughout your home.

- Start by lighting your candle and using the melted wax to close the jar.
- Put it in a visible location near your front door or on a mantelpiece to draw attention.

Good luck jar spell

INGREDIENTS:

- Bay Leaves
- Rice that's white
- A length of string or rope
- A speck of salt from the sea
- Citrine, amethyst, and labradorite are examples of crystals.
- A green candle.

METHOD:

These magic jars are wonderful to have on hand for those times when you require a smidgen of good fortune in any facet of your life. After you have thoughtfully placed all of your components inside the jar, capping it with the green candle wax, you should then consider the areas of your life in which you feel you might use some additional good fortune. This one would look great either next to your bed or inside your closet.

Calming spell jar

INGREDIENTS:

- Chamomile
- Lavender
- Gardenia
- Bergamot oil
- Moon water (place a bowl on your window ledge on a full moon)
- Amethyst, celestite, and malachite are examples of crystals.
- A candle in the color purple or blue

METHOD:

Try to make one of these calming magic jars if you find that anxiety and tension are constant companions in your life.

As always, feel free to pick and choose the components you need from this list of ingredients and make do with what you already have. These are merely ideas and pointers to help you make your magical spell jars; feel free to get creative!

After lighting your candle and taking some deep breaths, put the materials you've chosen into a jar that's been thoroughly cleaned. The inhalation of the essential oils and herbs contained in this jar will have a sedative and calming impact on your nervous system, making it the ideal thing to do.

The next step is to use some candle wax to seal the jar. Put this jar on your bedside table or the desk in your office to bring about a more relaxed vibration.

Sleep spell jar

INGREDIENTS:

- Lavender
- Chamomile
- Passionflower
- Valerian
- Lemon balm
- Some examples of crystals include amethyst, pure quartz, moonstone, and selenite.
- A white candle

METHOD:

It is recommended that you use sleep spell jars if you always awake in the middle of the night, have nightmares, or have problems falling or staying asleep. While creating this spell jar, put on some calming and serene music, like the sound of ocean waves or rain. Put all the components into the jar, and as you do so, give some thought to the goals you have set for your sleep.

Good health spell jar

INGREDIENTS:

- Rosemary
- A daisy Calendula
- Sage
- Black salt
- Amethyst, rose quartz, and black obsidian is examples of crystals.
- A green candle.

METHOD:

These health spell jars are the ideal item to make for yourself or someone else who requires a health boost or wants to ward off illness. You can make them for yourself or someone else.

- Gather all your components, and then arrange them in the jar in any way pleases you.
- Start by lighting your candle and seal the jar with green candle wax.
- Repeat an affirmation that you have chosen that relates to your state of health, such as "my body is nourished and healthy" or "I am well."
- Put this magical jar of spells somewhere that everyone can see in your home, or give it to a friend or family member who you

want to be robust and healthy.

Recipe for a money spell jar

I've had especially good luck with my money spell jars in the past few years. Here is one of my all-time favorite dishes from my kitchen.

WHAT YOU'LL NEED:

- A jar with a lid, preferably a mason jar but a glass jar with a metal lid will do.
- 3 coins
- paper and pen: I tear out pieces from brown paper bags OR pieces of parchment paper.
- Three examples are herbs that bring money, such as mint, basil, rosemary, and chamomile.
- Herb can dislodge obstructions; some examples include john the conqueror root and cayenne pepper.
- Sugar

CASTING INSTRUCTIONS FOR THE MONEY JAR SPELL:

- Purge your money jar's components by using whichever cleansing method strikes your fancy.
- Establish the tone. Turn on the radio, turn on the lights, etc.
- On the piece of paper, jot down your goals and objectives. I usually write my in three different places, but you can organize it however you like.
- Rotate the paper so that it faces you. Put it into the glass jar.

- After you have finished each plant, give it a light breath of air and place it in the jar. Imagine that money is coming to you steadily throughout the entire process.
- The next step is to place the three coins into the jar while reciting the following mantra: "by three times three, money flows freely to me for the utmost good of all."
- The herbs, coins, and paper should be covered with sugar almost to the top of the jar. When I'm finished, there will be space for shaking the contents, so I leave a little headroom at the top.
- Top the jar with the lid.
- Make a soft shaking motion with the jar while reciting the following money-drawing chant: "The roads are clear, there won't be any impediments, and money will come to me with the power of three times three. Therefore, let it be."
- Light a candle and place it atop the container. SAFETY FIRST! NEVER LEAVE UNATTENDED Objects or Areas!

I like to keep a candle burning on each of my jars for seven to nine days, during which time I pray continuously, shake the jar each day, and keep the flame burning.

Money spell jar or abundance spell jar

INGREDIENTS:

- Seeds (of any type)
- Bay Leaves
- Peppermint (the plant or essential oil)
- Giner de Chamomille (fresh or dried)
- A note or coin
- Crystals: jade or green aventurine
- Anything else that you consider to be a representation of abundance
- A sheet of paper on which your goals are written.
- A candle in either gold or green.

METHOD:

If you want to experience more abundance in your life or if you want to draw more money into your life, this money spell jar is for you.

- After placing every element in the jar, top it with gold or green candle wax.
- Consider what you are attracting, and imagine how you will feel and how your world will appear when operating from a place of complete alignment with the flow of abundance.

Business abundance jar spell

INGREDIENTS

- Lucky hand
- A bergamot-scented leaf plucked from a money tree (also known as orange mint)
- A note or several coins
- Crystals, including clear quartz, green aventurine, and green tourmaline
- A paper bearing the name of your company
- A candle that is either green or gold.

METHOD:

A business abundance magic jar is comparable to a money spell jar.

Still, its purpose is to assist you in attracting wealth and prosperity for your business rather than for yourself personally. Gather all of your components, and place them all in the jar, except your coins and the name of your company.

Put some flame in your candle. Write your company's name on a sheet of paper and place it next to your money. Alternatively, you might use one of the lovely business cards you've designed.

The next step is to put coins and a piece of paper into your jar after half-filling it with water. While doing this, think about what you want most for your company: more customers or sales, an incredible team, or a gorgeous office space.

Jars of spells to increase productivity

INGREDIENTS

- Sage
- Rosemary
- Peppermint
- Vanilla
- Cinnamon
- Cloves
- Tiger's eye, citrine, amazonite, and selenite are some examples of crystals.
- A yellow candle

METHOD:

This is the magic jar for you if you want to increase the amount of work you get done daily. Gather all of your ingredients, then store them in your jar. Turn on your candle and then fill the jar to the top with wax. Put this jar in the room where you conduct most of your work, whether that's your home office, a place of business, or somewhere that sees a lot of action, like the kitchen.

Jar containing protection spell

INGREDIENT:

- Salt of the sea with feathers
- Needles of a pine tree or a pine cone
- Oregano and/or rosemary
- Clover of white color
- Black tourmaline, black obsidian, or black jade are examples of crystals.
- A white candle

METHOD:

The protection jar is one of the most popular and extensively used magic jars. Put this jar in a place of prominence in your home to ward off harmful energies and safeguard your loved ones from harm.

After you have selected your components, place them in the jar, top it off with a white candle, and begin to recite a protection spell.

The perfect response would be, "We are protected" or "I am always safe in my home." Put your jar in a prominent location, such as the altar or the front door of your house.

Jar of curses for the defense of the home

We can all agree that protection is something that each of us requires. This need is always present. So without further ado, here is the formula for my home protection spell jar:

YOU WILL NEED THE FOLLOWING:

- A jar with a lid and photos of the people and/or pets you wish to protect.
- pen/marker
- Rosemary, thorns, pepper salt, and Witch's black salt all have defensive qualities.
- Cotton fluff can be obtained from an old stuffed animal that is no longer in use or from cotton or bedding that can be purchased from a fabric store. If you cannot locate this, you can substitute a plush fabric cut from an old t-shirt or blanket.

INSTRUCTIONS

- Cleanse all of Your Protection Jar Spell components Utilizing Whichever Method You Choose To Do So
- Establish the tone. Turn on the radio, turn on the lights, etc.
- On the reverse of the photograph, write down your objectives (s). In addition to that, I draw runes or other symbols of protection.
- Imagine a heavenly, white cloak of protection enveloping you

and/or your family members as you wrap the cotton fluff or the cloth around the photo(s). After that, put it in the jar.

- After you have finished each plant, give it a light breath of air and place it in the jar. Continue to picture or state your wishes to shield the person or persons within the jar from physical or spiritual harm.
- After that, sprinkle salt on it and say, "Guides and guardians protect my family and me through the power of three times three.." From every enemy, both in the bodily and the spiritual sense. Therefore, let it be."
- Put the lid on the jar's top.
- Repeat the prayer for protection provided earlier while holding the jar in your hands.
- On top of the jar, you should light a white or red candle. SAFETY FIRST! NEVER LEAVE UNATTENDED Objects or Areas!
- Then, put the jar containing the protection spell somewhere in your house accessible to all of your family members, if you included them (dining room, living room, etc.)

Spell jar to make people back off

INGREDIENTS

- Sage
- Basil
- Mint
- Black pepper
- Clove
- Water from rain
- Black tourmaline, clear quartz, and selenite are examples of crystals.
- A candle of a dark color

METHOD:

By using this magic jar, you will be able to drive away negative energy and maintain your environment upbeat and encouraging.

Put all ingredients in the jar, then sprinkle them over the rainwater at the top. Imagine that this is like a wash that removes any unpleasant vibes. Start the flame in your candle, then fill the jar to the top with the cooled candle wax. Put this jar of spells to work at the front door of your home or workplace to ward off negative energy and ensure that the space remains a positive, thriving environment.

Protection and breaking curses jar spells

Caution is advised, as the ancient protection spell discussed here is not necessarily the "fluffy bunny" part of witchcraft. I usually warn people that they will feel really uncomfortable once they do a powerful protection spell such as this one. This is one of the things that I make sure to do. Remember that practicing witchcraft isn't always attractive, unlike what you might see on Instagram; yet, what matters most is not its appearance but rather the POWER that it possesses.

WHAT YOU WILL NEED TO HAVE:

- A jar or container made of durable glass that has a lid
- An indeterminate quantity of sharp objects, such as pins, nails, needles, shattered glass, and other items, to "snag" the spirit.
- Personal effects include nail clippings, hair found on a hairbrush, pillow, etc.
- urine
- A chime candle is ideal, but a small black candle would do (the candle should NOT be in a holder).
- lighter/matches
- shovel

THE PROCEDURE TO FOLLOW:

- Before you even begin the spell, you should concentrate on your goal the ENTIRE time you are filling the bottle with the appropriate ingredients and capping it off.

- Place the pins or other sharp objects and the personal effects inside the bottle.
- Pour urine over the safety pins and other personal items (yeah, this is the gross part, but BRAIN UP, WITCH!)
- Put the lid back on the jar or bottle to seal it.
- Burn the black candle atop the container, but do it carefully! Don't go away and forget about the candle for too long. It would help if you made it such that the wax drips onto the top of the jar. Burn the candle right down to the bottom.) This ratifies your goals and objectives.
- You can give the bottle extra "oomph" by "heating it " by holding it over an open bonfire, but this step is completely discretionary and is not essential.
- Create a hole on your land that is approximately one foot deep. It works well either by the window of your bedroom or by the door of the front entrance.
- Put your witch bottle in the ground and cover it with melted candle wax. Throughout the entire process, you keep picturing any evil being sucked into the witch bottle and confined there for all of the time.
- Put down the bottle of witchcraft. Never dig it back up!
- The purpose of the spell is to provide tremendous protection as well as to break the hex.

Lemon freezer spell:

For hundreds of years, lemons have been essential in various magical activities. They exude a fundamentally purifying energy and prefer the moon, the feminine, and water due to their innate connection with these things. They are also employed in charms that are cast to make a person avoid touch with the person casting the charm. It's the same reaction you'd get from someone if you gave them lemons to eat: they'd probably gag and refuse to even taste them. As a consequence of this, if you require something to rid yourself of a person who is causing you annoyance, you can use this lemon freezer spell to send them on their way after freezing them off:

WHAT YOU'LL NEED TO GET STARTED:

- a Lemon (1 whole)
- Toothpicks and needles could be used (4-6)
- Paper
- Pen

- Or a container made of plastic.
- That of your freezer.

USAGE INSTRUCTIONS FOR THE LEMON FREEZER SPELL:

- Gather your tools and supplies because there is nothing to clean before you start.
- Play music that inspires you to chase them away or makes you feel comfortable and secure.
- Write down the person's name or situation on a short paper.
- As you fold the paper three times in the other direction, visualize the person or circumstance leaving your life forever.
- Cut the lemon in half lengthwise, but stop short of cutting through. Just enough to provide room for the piece of paper to be put.
- Be careful not to stab yourself when using needles or toothpicks to close the open cut in the lemon.
- Put it in a plastic bag or container and place it at the bottom and back of your freezer. The freezer can "freeze them out" or make them hostile so that they will avoid you out of discomfort.
- You should clean the pen if you plan to use it again soon or later (run it through smoke, etc.)
- Remove the packaged lemon from the freezer after they are no longer a part of your life, and throw it away in a location far

from your home and property. AT NO POINT SHOULD YOU UNWRAP THE LEMON.

Freezer binding spell

When a house alarm and a large canine companion are not sufficient to deter an intruder, sometimes we could use a tiny bit of magic to protect ourselves from harm. This quick-fix spell for binding with ice and snow works quite effectively. It is also beneficial if the individual who has to be bound is hurting a family member or a close friend. You can cast this magic for them only if they permit you.

What You Will Need to Have:

- Or a container made of plastic.
- Use of a pen and paper (optional: picture of the offender)
- Water
- Freezer
- Herbs for binding and expelling, such as rue, thorns, or pepper, can be added as an option.

How to do the freezer binding spell: instructions

As you gather your resources, remember that the offender will soon be stopped from hurting anyone else.

- On the piece of paper you have, write the offender's name.
- Fold the piece of paper three times in the opposite direction from you and tell yourself, "You are not allowed to damage me or anyone nearby." by three times three's strength. (To intensify the impact, repeat this three times.) Let it therefore

be.
- Place the paper or photo in a bag or container made of plastic.
- Fill the container with water and the herbs of your choice, and then declare, "With the ancient power of water, you will never come near me and me again."
- Close the bag's lid and declare that "it is finished." Then, place it in the freezer.

Remember to remove the spell once the intended victim has been kept from hurting you or your loved ones. I suggest you bury the plastic bag's contents, including the photo, paper, and contents, far from your property and throw the bag into the trash. Burying plastic on the earth is not a good idea.

EVERYTHING ABOUT CORRESPONDENCE

In real life, there isn't a comprehensive correspondence list, and when you're working with images and words, things have the potential to become muddled — or, if you use them effectively, they can have potent results! Consider what the images and phrases you choose to work with mean to YOU before making any selections, regardless of the project's purpose.

The following is a small selection of the many things and components that can be placed within witch bottles.

- Crystals
- Dried herbs
- Spices, either ground or in their fully dried form

- Dried fruit and vegetables
- Essential oils
- Water and the waters of magic
- Shells
- Coins
- Bones
- Beads

A witch bottle can be filled with anything left undisturbed for an extended period inside an airtight container.

Great strength components for witch bottles

Depending on the ritual's goal, you may also include other elements in addition to personal items and sharp instruments, such as the following:

- herbs connected to the purpose of your gathering
- stones and stony objects
- bones
- feathers
- glitter
- blessed oils
- moon, or the water of sanctity
- photographs and/or pieces of paper with the goals written on them
- coins

- buttons

Additional non-essential personal things

- sugar
- salt
- liquor
- offerings

Various groups to select items from

It's most convenient for me to select items from the following groups:

A piece of one's own

It is essential to your spell that you use a photograph, hair, nail clippings, blood, or some other personal object. You might also utilize a name written down on a piece of paper. This should be of the person you are performing the spell on; for example, if you are casting the magic for yourself, you would use a photo of yourself, an item that belonged to you, or your name. If you were casting the magic for a friend or on someone else (such as a spell to convince a bully to stop bothering you, for example), you would use their photo, name, or an item that belonged to them.

Intention or prayer expressed in writing

You can write a note to a deity asking for their assistance in your jar magic if you want to request their assistance and involve them in the spell. Since there is a lot of power in words, I usually find it beneficial to write my intention on anything and then slide it into the jar. I hope that whatever I ask for will come true.

Liquids

Urine is used to protecting jars and jars that are used to break a curse. However, urine can also be added to spells to manipulate other people. In general, the bottle should hold some liquid, but the specific liquid you pick will depend on the purpose of the endeavor.

Vinegar can be used as a curse to harm others or 'ruin' something. Be aware that vinegar jars have the potential to burst, so avoid filling them up and always store them with the lids tightly covered in fabric or towels (unless you plan on burying them).

When you need someone or anything to do what you want them to, you can use honey, sugar water, or another sort of nectar. This is because you would want to "sweeten" their temperament if you were trying to make friends with them, trying to be more persuasive, trying to soothe over bruised sentiments, etc.

When you want to rid yourself of negativity or evil forces, or when you want to start over with a "clean slate," you can use ammonia to "cleanse" or "purge" your environment.

WARNING: Never light candles on ammonia, and keep ammonia jars away from heat sources. Ammonia can explode and cause fires, so never do either.

Tinctures, infusions, oils, and various other preparations can each serve various functions, including blessing blessings upon an individual for their health or prosperity. Naturally, it would help if you chose anything based on the intention you have in mind. For instance, a tincture, infusion, or oil prepared from money-drawing plants such as cinnamon or mint could be included in a spell intended to bring financial success to its practitioner.

Water can be utilized, but I wouldn't recommend drinking it on its own very often. You might try making a herbal infusion with it to give it a little kick-start. This would be the very minimum. To the extent that it is possible, I would recommend avoiding drinking ordinary tap water. However, I believe that water that has been strongly salted and blessed can be beneficial for purifying purposes.

Solids

Also, as there are many various liquids, there are many different solids from which you can choose. You have a lot of room for creativity with this! The following are some examples that illustrate this point:

- Jar spells typically involve using corroded nails and broken pieces of Glass to lift a curse.
- The caster might add cat and dog hair to the mixture to break up a relationship. This would cause the individuals to fight like "cats and dogs," but you should remember that this could be unethical.
- A love-drawing spell cast in a jar can include the addition of glitter or confetti in the shape of hearts. You may also tie a ribbon around the entire jar to keep your love for someone close to you or to bond them to you.

- If your jar spell involves money, you might want to incorporate some coins (preferably with the year of your birth printed on them).
- If I wanted to get through my writer's block, I might cast a spell using a jar with a small pencil and a roll of paper wrapped around it.

Crystals and medicinal herbs

Crystals and herbs are two things that are easily accessible but also have a significant amount of magical power. They can carry the energy you wish to put into your spell, and you can locate a variety of them anyplace. They are also easy to find. If you are new to dealing with herbs and crystals, I have included a handy reference sheet below that you may refer to whenever you need it.

The more experience you have working with herbs and crystals and getting a sense of how they behave, the more adept you will become at casting spells.

All you need to do is utilize your brain to consider the kinds of things that emit the energy that you are looking to cultivate as a plant. If they have a special significance for you, then your spell will work much more effectively with them (vs. only using items commonly associated with your goal).

Note: Keep in mind that you need to purify and consecrate the objects you intend to place inside the spell jar in the same manner as you purified and consecrated the magic jar itself. It is less likely that your spell will be successful in

helping you achieve your objective if the objects you have selected are not pure on a spiritual level (that is, on an energy level).

Intent	Crystals, Gems, Metals	Herbs, Flowers, Roots
Banishing	obsidian, jet, black tourmaline, smokey quartz	clove, dragon's blood, garlic, hot pepper
Binding	jet	agrimony, knotweed, spiderwort, witch hazel
Communication	sodalite, tiger eye, turquoise	mint, orris root
Curse-Breaking	onyx, clear quartz, selenite	angelica, bloodroot, boneset, mandrake, salt, sage, rue
Fertility	agate, emerald, garnet, malachite, peridot	apple, cucumber, fig, ivy

Health	agate, amethyst, jade, sunstone	coriander, dogwood, eucalyptus, galangal root, ginger, rosemary, sage, thyme
Intellect	aventurine, flourite	benzoin, dittany of Crete, nugmeg, rosemary,
Love	amber, calcite, copper emerald, lapis lazuli, moonstone, rose quartz	Adam & Eve root, apple, basil, beet, catnip, clove, laurel, lavender, marjoram, rose
Money	gold, malachite, moss agate, pearl	cinnamon, ginger, orange, patchouly, vervain

Peace	amazonite, blue lace agate, rhodocrosite, silver	cumin, lavender, violet
Productivity	fuschite, gold, hematite, ruby	allspice, oregano, vanilla
Protection	amber, carnelian, citrine, malachite, petrified wood	angelica, cypress, frankincense, mugwort, sandalwood, wormwood
Psychic Abilities	Iolite, jet, malachite, moonstone, quartz, turquoise, silver	acacia, gardenia, mugwort, tuberose, yarrow
Relationships	moss agate, pearl, peridot, rhodocrosite, sapphire, turquoise	pansy, rose, valerian

*Please be aware that the following list is not intended to be comprehensive; however, it should offer you a fair number of ideas to get you started.

Essential tools for spells

When choosing what to put on your witch altar, a good place to start is with the vibe and energy you want to bring into your life and what helps you connect with your spiritual side.

The second stage is getting objects to help you feel and project the mood you want. Whatever you feel is suitable. Anything that immediately appeals to you.

Setting up all your tools in one spot is a good idea. Many witches will store everything on an altar that has been dedicated. They will do moon rituals, work on spells here, and perhaps even engage in yoga or meditation.

The following tools are normal to see on a witch's altar:

- A candle or some incense
- Wand
- Athame
- Your shadows book
- the four elements represented by objects
- Cauldron
- Chalice

- crystals or rocks
- Useful substances
- plants and flowers
- Herbs and spices, whether fresh or dried
- Altar linen
- Oracle or tarot cards
- Quill or a pen
- deities' statues
- images of beloved people or motivational pictures
- holy books
- Notations or affirmations written by hand
- Jewelry
- Mirror (excellent for abundance) (great for abundance)
- Money

Elements

The following is a list of additional items that could be considered candidates to symbolize each of the four elements:

- East (air): A dreamcatcher, feather, pen, or wing.
- South (fire): A candle, a smudge stick, or a lit match.
- The term "west" can refer to a bowl, chalice, or vase containing water, shells, or salt (water).
- The direction of the north on Earth is symbolic of a crystal, some mud, a plant or flower, a stone, or a bone.

Color meanings for candles

The candle is a wonderful religious object to set anywhere, But how do you determine which color to choose to place on your altar?

Here are the meanings associated with each color.

White: Reset, find truth, serenity, quiet, harmony, thankfulness, and healing. Make a connection with your own and the moon's goddess energy.

Black: Drive away bad energies, release blocked or stagnant energy, break a harmful habit, end an unfavorable circumstance or relationship, and undo curses or hexes.

Red: Increases hunger, lust or attraction, flirting, uterine wisdom, confidence (especially sexual confidence), willpower, fortitude, bravery, and resolve; it also attracts luck and aids at the beginning of a new beginning.

Pink: Self-love, coziness, companionship, happiness, romance, affection, closeness, and empathy. Heal yourself or a relationship, extend forgiveness, and nurture a new relationship.

Blue: Enhance your ability to communicate, concentrate, or remember; and heal and reach out to your higher self (emotionally or spiritually). Get motivated and unleash your inner Creatrix.

Green: Generosity, abundance, manifestation, success, money, good fortune, and a physical connection to mother nature.

Brown: Establish a solid foundation, maintain equilibrium, foster trust, deflect conflict, and cultivate empathy.

Purple: Helps you to meditate, broaden your spiritual consciousness, activate your third eye, hone your psychic abilities, and learn more about yourself.

Orange: Effective for networking, career changes, taking the initiative, quitting bad habits, and letting go of addictions. Additionally, it enables you to live a life filled with greater play, vigor, and delight.

Yellow: Overcome mental challenges, achieve clarity, sharpen intelligence and attention, stoke creativity and optimism, and adopt a more rational perspective.

Plants and flowers

Fresh or dried flowers and plants can provide color and life to your witch altar while incorporating the element of earth. Because they are employed in many spells and healing potions, herbs are also necessary for any kitchen or green witch.

Here are some common flowers and herbs, along with their witchcraft-related meanings.

- Aloe: Restorative, protective, and adoring
- Basil: Warm regards
- Bay: Praise
- Chamomile: Restraint
- Chrysanthemum: Optimism
- Coriander: Untapped value
- Integrity, cumin
- Youthful crocuses
- Daffodil: Consider
- Daisy: Hope and innocence
- Dill: Dispels evil spirits
- Fennel: Generous
- Insincerity, Fern
- Holly: Joy and celebration
- Honeysuckle: Loving ties
- Fertility: hyacinth

- Ivy: Continuity and friendship
- Sweet love, Jasmine
- Lavender: Love and goodness
- Lemon balm: Condolences
- Lilac: Youthful joy
- Virtue: mint
- Myrtle: Commitment and genuine love
- Oak: Stability
- Oregano: Substance
- Pansy: Opinions
- Parsley: Holiday
- Pine: Modesty
- Poppies: Solace
- Rose: Romance, ardor, and love.
- Rosemary: Thinking back
- Sage: Resurrection, immortality, and wisdom
- Sorrel: Feeling
- Tarragon: Persistent appeal
- Thyme: fortitude & fortitude
- Violet: Faithfulness, commitment, and loyalty

Crystals

Crystals are a great way to enhance your witch altar and simultaneously add the element of air. They can be used in baths, spellwork, and moon ceremonies. They are highly versatile. Hold them in your hands while you meditate, or lie down and place them on your forehead or your heart while having the most imaginative dreams.

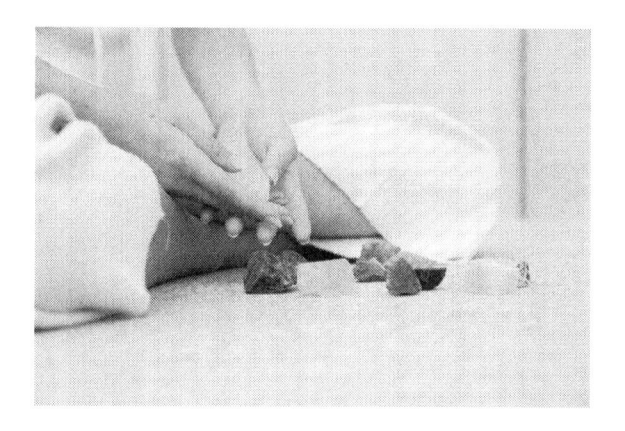

The most well-known crystals and their meanings are listed here. So that you are aware, try not to get too caught up in these connotations since it is quite easy to do so. I suggest seeing photos of crystals online or in stores to determine which ones you find appealing. Take this as a sign of what you most urgently require right now.

- Amethyst: Intuition and serenity
- Amazonite: Hope and intuition
- Clarity, purity, and peace symbolized by aquamarine
- Carnelian will enhance your libido and the root and sacral chakras.
- Celestite: Upbeat and inspiring
- Citrine: Rejuvenate, purify, and bring prosperity
- Quartz crystals: energize
- Fire agate symbolizes bravery and defense.

- Green jade: emotional harmony, fortune, and success
- Moonstone: The Goddess, new beginnings, and feminine energy
- Obsidian: Psychic purification and defense
- Red jasper: Stimulate and ground
- Rose-colored quartz: Peace and love
- Selenite: Harmony, ethereality, clarity, and light.
- Tiger eye: Individual strength
- Tourmaline: Strengthens and lessens fear

CONCLUSION

This book aims to provide beginner-friendly spell jar recipes and the act of casting a spell so you can better their practice.

You must maintain an open mind to the possibilities of what you want throughout these spell casting and imagine if everything in your life has already occurred. It won't until you think it can happen. Have faith that you will get what you require. Even when pursuing more, expressing gratitude for what you already have is vital.

Spells, especially those involving manifestation, function better when cast for oneself than for another. We already struggle to understand our desires, never mind those of others.

You have now learned more about your true self, beliefs, desires, and motives, as well as the Universe, the more spellwork you do.

Manufactured by Amazon.ca
Bolton, ON